UNIVERSITY OF NEW MEXICO PUBLICATIONS IN ECONOMICS

NUMBER ONE

NEWTONIAN CLASSICISM AND DARWINIAN INSTITUTIONALISM

A Study of Change in Economic Theory

DAVID HAMILTON

GREENWOOD PRESS, PUBLISHERS
WESTPORT, CONNECTICUT

Library of Congress Cataloging in Publication Data

Hamilton, David Boyce, 1918-
Newtonian classicism and Darwinian institutionalism.

Reprint of the ed. published by University of New Mexico Press, Albuquerque, which was issued as no. 1 of University of New Mexico publications in economics.
Bibliography: p.
1. Economics—History. I. Title. II. Series: New Mexico. University. University of New Mexico publications in economics; no. 1.
[HB87.H26 1975] 330.1 73-8558
ISBN 0-8371-6969-0

Originally published in 1953 by the University of New Mexico Press, Albuquerque

Reprinted in 1975 by Greenwood Press
A division of Congressional Information Service, Inc.,
88 Post Road West, Westport, Connecticut 06881

Library of Congress Catalog Card Number 73-8558

ISBN 0-8371-6969-0

Printed in the United States of America

10 9 8 7 6 5 4 3 2

ACKNOWLEDGMENTS

For my early interest in institutional economics I owe a debt to Professors F. D. Tyson and R. A. Dixon of the University of Pittsburgh. Professor C. E. Ayres of the University of Texas is responsible for developing this early interest into a more acute appreciation. To the latter I am additionally indebted for the time and insight given to the organization and presentation of this inquiry and for having patience beyond the call of duty. To Professor E. E. Hale, also of the University of Texas, I am grateful for a careful reading of the entire manuscript and for many helpful criticisms and suggestions. I want to thank Professor Joseph Dorfman of Columbia University for having read the entire manuscript and for helpful criticism. I also want to thank Professor Mervyn Crobaugh of the University of New Mexico for having read the manuscript. To Professor Julian Duncan of the University of New Mexico I owe a debt of gratitude that cannot be easily repaid. The original manuscript has benefited very much from the skillful editing of Barry Stevens, formerly of the University of New Mexico. Needless to say, all shortcomings in the study are those of the author.

I wish to thank the following publishers and authors for permission to quote from copyrighted publications: University of North Carolina Press from *The Theory of Economic Progress* by C. E. Ayres; Columbia University Press from *The Philosophy of Thorstein Veblen* by Stanley Daugert; Yale University Press from *The Heavenly City of the Eighteenth Century Philosophers* by Carl Becker; University of Pennsylvania Press from *Social Darwinism in America* by Richard Hofstadter; Macmillan and Company, Ltd., and St. Martin's Press Inc. from *The Nature and Significance of Economic Science* by Lionel Robbins; Prentice-Hall, Inc. from *A History of Economic Thought* by Eric Roll and from *Modern Economic Thought* by Allan Gruchy; Henry Holt and Co. from *Human Nature and Conduct* by John Dewey; Penguin Books, Ltd. from *What Happened in History* by V. Gordon Childe; J. M. Clark from *Essentials of Economic Theory* by J. B. Clark; Augustus M. Kelley, Inc. from *Karl Marx and the Close of His System* by Eugen von Böhm-Bawerk and from *The Backward Art of Spending Money* by Wesley Mitchell; The Macmillan Company from *The Rise of American Civilization* by C. A. and M. R. Beard and from "Institutions" and from

"Organization, Economic" by Walton Hamilton in *The Encyclopedia of the Social Sciences;* McGraw-Hill Book Company, Inc. from *Economic Institutions and Cultural Change* by Russell A. Dixon and from *Economics and Cultural Change* by Russell A. Dixon and E. Kingman Eberhart; Charles Scribner's Sons from *The Building of Cultures* by Roland B. Dixon; The Beacon Press from *Magic, Science and Religion* by Bronislaw Malinowski; The University of Chicago Press from "The Development of Hoxie's Economics" by Walton Hamilton in *The Journal of Political Economy,* Vol. XXIV; The Viking Press from *The Instinct of Workmanship and the State of the Industrial Arts, Imperial Germany and the Industrial Revolution, The Place of Science in Modern Civilization,* and *The Nature of Peace and the Terms of Its Perpetuation*—all by Thorstein Veblen; Alfred A. Knopf, Inc. from "Keynes, The Economist (3)" by Paul Sweezey in *The New Economics* edited by Seymour Harris; Farrar, Straus and Young, Inc. from *The Science of Culture* by Leslie White; Houghton Mifflin Co. from *The Making of the Modern Mind* by John H. Randall, Jr.; Harper and Brothers from *Economic Analysis* by Kenneth Boulding and from *Capitalism, Socialism and Democracy* by Joseph A. Schumpeter; American Economic Association from "Fifty Years' Development in Ideas of Human Nature and Motivation" by C. E. Ayres in *The American Economic Review,* Vol. XXVI, and from "Roundtable Conference on Institutional Economics" by J. M. Clark in *The American Economic Review,* Vol. XXII; Harcourt Brace and Company from *The General Theory of Employment, Interest and Money* by J. M. Keynes.

DAVID HAMILTON

Albuquerque
July, 1953

PREFACE

If any prospective reader of this book is looking for a calm, objective, historical essay in economic history—as he might if he were guided by the title—let him be warned now. He will be sorely disappointed. This is a controversial book, written from a particular point of view by a man who might well be classified as a disciple. It is always controversial and sometimes polemical. It is never calm, cool, or dispassionate.

As such, it is safe to predict, reaction to it will be more in the nature of praise and condemnation than of careful assessment. In fact, it is hard to imagine a reviewer taking a detached attitude toward the thesis here presented; and it is fairly certain that the author would be sorely disappointed if that were to happen.

But such characterization of the book is not a condemnation. Quite the reverse. We grow and make progress only as partisan points of view are forcibly expressed and jolt us out of our complacent acceptance of orthodoxy. Further it is only through discussion pro and con of ideas that they come, finally, to be shaped and welded and sharpened into the useable tools we so desperately need in an era where ideas are recognized as essential weapons. Hence we should all be eager to put our ideas up for such discussion and reshaping, as I am sure this author is.

This book is written from the "Institutional" point of view —that branch of economic thought which attacks institutions, as it defines them, as the brakes on progress and hails technology as the shining knight in armor who leads us forward in spite of our worst efforts. Early the author denies his orthodoxy; gladly he admits to heresy. He assures us that he, and the faith he represents, fall well outside the main stream of economic theory from Adam Smith through J. M. Keynes. In a slightly sectarian aside, he also rules out those who would call themselves "Institutionalists" but who are not true followers of Thorstein Veblen and the men who have sought to build their theories on Veblen's fundamental theses.

Classical economic theory, of course, is the bête noire against which this author's lance is driven. It is granted that the orthodox classicists and the neo-classicists have won the field, and have even crowed in their triumph that what was good in "Institutionalism" has been integrated into their system, but it is also hotly charged that they have fooled no one but themselves. And if they do not believe it, then just let them try to work their theories of dynamics!

For, Hamilton argues, it is just here, in theories of dynamics, that the whole classical theoretical structure is found to be without foundation. And this comes about because the classicists stopped thinking with Newton whereas the Institutionalists moved on forward and accepted Darwin. This makes all the difference between accepting a mechanistic and essentially static concept and embracing the evolutionary, cumulative, cultural outlook which alone is consonant with life and scholarship today.

In this sense, this book is an essay in the sociology of knowledge. It sees economic thought reflecting the dominant mental climates of two different eras, just as the sociologists have insisted for the past two or three decades happens with regularity. This thesis also opens our thinking to the possibility that in a new era there will be a new economic thought which will be then hailed as the true explanation of what was seen only obscurely in the past.

Perhaps it was out of his study of sociology as well as his study of economics under recognized exponents of the Institutional school that the thesis for this book was derived. At any rate, it is safe to say that the book does take one step toward an integration of economics and sociology; as, indeed, is true of Institutionalism in general. A British publisher some years ago published a volume on Veblen as a sociologist. This cross-fertilization of the fields of social science is a fine thing, or so it seems to me. This is not to say that I would approve of all that is here said. In fact, I would find myself forced to disagree with much of it. But it is an honest book, honestly written with no pretense of not saying what the author believes and is ready to fight for. Those who wish to hurl challenges are respectfully referred to the author.

HARRY ESTILL MOORE

University of Texas

FOREWORD

There is no problem that has given rise to more disagreement among economists than the problem of economic change. Not only is there much disagreement as to the nature of economic change, but there is also a great lack of unanimity of opinion as to how to deal with the problem. As Professor Hamilton so ably points out, all economists will agree that their analyses should include a study of economic change. The main disagreement arises over what should be included in this concept. Change may be considered from a mechanical, static point of view or from an evolutionary, dynamic approach. Whether the economist takes the essence of economic change to be mere mechanical motion or, instead, significant evolutionary development has much to do with his views on the nature and scope of economic science. Where the economist takes the former approach to economic change, economics becomes a narrow discipline which is mainly concerned with the study of economic equilibrium. Professor Hamilton explains that this observation is equally applicable to Keynesian and Marshallian economics, both of which take the goal of economic analysis to be a concern with some kind of equilibrium. Where the economist considers change to be a matter of growth, development, and evolutionary expansion, economics turns out to be a broad social science which is more capable of coming to grips with the major economic issues of the twentieth century. This is the provocative conclusion that emerges from Professor Hamilton's study of how orthodox and institutionalist economists analyze the problem of economic change.

Three conditions account for the failure of economists to make room in their analyses for a broad study of evolutionary change. First, economics was a well-established science long before evolutionary concepts had become a part of the intellectual furniture of most men. By origin and tradition the science of economics is therefore non-evolutionary. Secondly, many economists have been proud of the fact that their science is more exact than other social sciences. The insistence on making and keeping economics exact has tended to cause economists not to cultivate those areas where the mathematical approach is not fruitful. As a result the scope of economics has been unduly narrowed to accommodate those who refuse to go beyond equilibrium analysis. Since economic change in its broadest sense cannot be satisfactorily reduced to the Procrustean limits of mathematical economics, the non-literary or "exact" economists have largely disregarded problems of economic change by making the study of economic change little more than an excursion into the field of comparative statics.

The third reason why economists have tended to ignore economic change of an evolutionary or developmental nature is that a study of this type of change has not always been welcomed by certain groups in the community. As Wesley C. Mitchell has pointed out, while change is the order of the day in the field of natural science, this is not true of economics and other social sciences. Economic changes frequently alter the institutional structure of society, and also the gainful opportunities of many groups. Studies of economic change have not been fostered, in some instances, for fear that such studies would hasten the process of economic and social reconstruction. It can hardly be denied that the very close connection between economic change and economic reform has tended to push the study of economic change into the "sociological penumbra" of Lionel Robbins and other so-called orthodox economists, where many significant economic matters have been conveniently impounded and soon forgotten.

The failure of economists to give adequate attention to the role of change in economic affairs has had two most unfortunate consequences. The first consequence relates to the field of economics education, while the second is concerned with the field of economic policy making. In the field of economics education the failure of current basic textbooks to give the student an adequate interpretation of the evolving American economic system is most lamentable. Recent years have witnessed a veritable spate of new economics textbooks all of which succeed very well in not conveying to the beginner any broad understanding of the dynamic, changing American economy. The typical textbook now adds some new Keynesian analytical tools to the arsenal of well-worn Marshallian tools, but fails to make the student realize that he is a participant in a great economic process which, like Alfred N. Whitehead's "event," incorporates something of the past, present, and future. As long as economists continue to give inadequate attention to problems of economic change they will continue to be long on mere tool-building and short on significant economic interpretation. A proper appreciation of the nature of economic change would make economists realize that tool-making should be only preliminary to realistic economic interpretation, which takes as its central fact the rapidly-changing structure and function of the modern industrialized economy.

The second unfortunate consequence of giving inadequate attention to economic change is that much economics provides an unsatisfactory basis for economic policy making. In an age of swiftly moving events and highly disruptive changes, such as our age, there is an obligation on the part of social scientists to submit this changing, developing age to close scrutiny, so that less-detached people in the world of politics may have the full benefit of whatever social-science generalizations may be worked out. There is today too much of a gap between economic theory and economic policy. The reason for this gap is found in part in the unwillingness of the majority of economists to substitute an evolutionary approach for the inherited static, Newtonian point of departure.

Professor Hamilton has traced the origins and development of these two points of departure in the field of economics by drawing attention to how economists have dealt with the problem of economic change since the time of Adam Smith. He has shown how differences in the treatment of economic change by economists show up in their discussions of human nature, social organization, and economic progress. Professor Hamilton's study of the concept of change in economic science serves two highly important purposes. It draws attention to the fact that there is a basic intellectual incompatibility between Newtonian and Darwinian economics which no shallow eclecticism will ever be able to gloss over. His study is also a challenge to economists to question some of the inherited preconceptions on which they seek to erect the structure of their thought systems. Economics is a branch of human thought which, like all cultural products, should be a reflection of the social process of unending change.

It is high time that economists in general came to recognize this simple but basic fact. Professor Hamilton's stimulating analysis should greatly aid economists in arriving at this fundamental understanding of the nature of their science.

ALLAN G. GRUCHY

University of Maryland

CONTENTS

NEWTONIAN CLASSICISM AND DARWINIAN INSTITUTIONALISM

INTRODUCTION

To many contemporary economists institutional economics is something that came into the stream of economic thought, made some valuable but minor contributions, and then disappeared from economic inquiry. One student who has taken this position has referred to the work of institutionalists as "the 'Institutional' episode,"[1] an attitude in which the more charitable members of the orthodox sect of political economy concur. To the less charitably minded, the contributions of institutionalism are looked upon as points of possible contamination that fortunately were escaped and so have left unmarred the pristine purity of the orthodox stream.[2]

The contradictory nature of these two positions indicates that something is not clear. There is a further lack of clarity in the relegation of institutionalism to an inferior role while the outcry against it in orthodox circles continues. One does not become perturbed over something which is of no consequence.

Perhaps even more significant is the fact that there have been at least five serious works in institutional economics in the past six years, each of which stresses differences between orthodoxy and institutionalism. This would seem to indicate that there are institutionalists today, in spite of the opinions of the orthodox, and that they do not believe that institutionalism is buried in the graveyard of discarded economic systems, nor that its doctrines have been absorbed by the current classical economics.

The importance of the appearance of five volumes of theory in six years might seem to be questionable, but it should be

1 Lewis H. Haney, *History of Economic Thought,* New York, Macmillan, 1936, p. 748. See also John M. Ferguson, *Landmarks of Economic Thought,* New York, Longmans, Green and Co., 1938, p. 269; Eric Roll, *A History of Economic Thought,* New York, Prentice-Hall, 1946, pp. 498-500.

2 See in Joseph Dorfman, *Thorstein Veblen and His America,* New York, Viking, 1940, comment of Joseph Schumpeter quoted on pp. 499-500.

remembered that apart from Veblen, whose published works appeared over a period of forty years, and one volume by John R. Commons in the mid-thirties, there have been no books—prior to these five recent volumes—purporting to deal with institutional theory *per se*. In the thirties there was much talk, in vague terms, about the significance of institutional economics—"the new economics"—but nothing was published. Under these circumstances, the publication of five volumes in the past six years can reasonably be called a resurgence.

Institutionalism represents—to institutionalists at least—a revolutionary way of observing economic phenomena. It is not complementary to classical economics, merely completing the sociological aspects of an otherwise logically tight system. Nor does institutionalism present a body of maxims such as all the varieties of classical economics have done. Institutionalism and classicism stem from different backgrounds and have different antecedents; they are products of antithetical ways of thinking about economic behavior. Where classicism was developed out of eighteenth-century Newtonianism, institutionalism is a product of the Darwinian revolution of the nineteenth century. The difference between them, therefore, is not simply a matter of one representing a static or crosscut view of the economy and the other representing a historical view. Their different backgrounds give to each its particular flavor and the flavors do not blend.

The institutionalist claims that classical economics is static and thus is not in tune with modern social thought, i.e., it is pre-Darwinian, as Veblen puts it. The classicist counters with the statement that he does deal with change in his economic dynamics. If, then, a major difference exists between the two schools in economic theory with regard to change, the difference must be found in their concepts of change.

The hypothesis to be demonstrated is that classicism clings to a Newtonian concept of change and that this concept is ramified throughout its body of doctrine; that it can be shown that the classical concepts of human nature, the social universe, and progress all reflect Newtonian change; and that all of these fit into a general pattern of Newtonianism. This concept is that of a mechanical and repetitive change in accordance with rather fixed eternal laws of social mechanics.

In contrast to this concept of change is that of the institutionalist. Embodied in institutional theory is a Darwinian concept of cumulative and constant evolution in which change is developmental, not mechanical. This concept can be shown to characterize the institutionalist's perception of human nature, social organization, and progress as part of the pattern of evolutionary change.

With these different concepts of change, there is necessarily a significant difference in the nature of what is conceived as economic theory, and it is from the concepts of change and of what changes that much of the difference arises between these two schools of economic theory.

Both of these concepts are themselves a product of the evolution of the idea of change. All people at all times have necessarily had some concept of change, but this concept has been subject to a process of cumulative development. As man's tools for the observation of change have improved, his concept of change and of what changes has expanded, and where once animism was rife in ideas of change, today change is viewed as a non-teleological, cumulative, and continuous process.

Since classical economics has been clearly recognized as a specific body of doctrine, and classical economists are easily differentiated by adherence to this doctrine, it is not necessary at this point to discuss what is meant by these designations beyond mentioning that for purposes of this study "classical economists" are all those in the main stream of economic thought from Adam Smith to J. M. Keynes. Occasionally, for clarity, some of these will be referred to as neoclassicists or Keynesian, but they all, nevertheless, belong to the classical phylum.

Institutional economics, on the other hand, is not so clearly defined, as this has been a classification into which all economics has been placed which does not obviously bear the classical stamp. Minor dissent from the classical fold has sometimes earned for the dissenter an institutionalist niche. Statistical research has been classified as institutionalism, and long statistical analyses of prices and price movements in specific industries have been called institutional economics. In some cases a sociological approach to economics has been called institutional. One of the most widely held concepts of institutionalism is that which identifies it with empirical research and the description of "economic reality." Institutionalism is believed by the orthodox to be non-theoretical and descriptive, while classical economics is held to be theoretical.

It is therefore necessary to state that for purposes of this study institutional economics will be limited to the work of those economists in the United States who have been clearly recognized as institutional economists. Institutionalism will be taken as that economic theory developed by Veblen and those American economists who have largely adhered to the outlook and major premises of Veblen. John Gambs in his reappraisal of institutional economics followed the same procedure.[3] As here defined, institutionalism has been almost exclusively an American development. Indeed, one recent writer considers it "the American contribution" to economic theory.[4]

It may be objected that the rather wide use of generalized statements on institutionalism in this work are not justified, in that no individual institutionalist held a particular idea unqualifiedly. This objection is not, however, considered sufficiently valid to require qualification in all instances. There is no intention to imply that all institutionalists held each concept discussed. Evidence of the difference of opinion on the part of classicists, who do not all hold to each and every facet of what passes as classical theory, is to be found in the journal discussions of the finer points of orthodox economics, yet this divergence of opinion does not preclude making generalized statements about classicism. In like manner, generalized statements about institutionalism may be made, albeit there are specific deviants from the norm. Too often in the past institutionalism has been approached individual by individual; no common ground has been found among them, and this has led to the contention of some critics that what passes as institutionalism is the product of a herd of dissidents seeking company in misery. One of the aims of this inquiry is to show that there is a well-established body of economic thought sufficiently similar in outlook to be given the title "Institutionalism."

---

3 John Gambs, *Beyond Supply and Demand,* New York, Columbia, 1946, p. 1.
4 Allan Gruchy, *Modern Economic Thought,* New York, Prentice-Hall, 1947.

I

CHANGE OR NO CHANGE

By the second decade of this century, the work of Veblen had made some impact on economic theorists and there had developed a group of prominent economists such as Hoxie, Mitchell, and Hamilton who were proclaiming a "new economics." This new economics was held to be different from the traditional doctrine in several significant ways, and it was expected that a revolutionary change in economic theory was in prospect. Exactly what kind of change was implied is not easily determined, for the differences between the two schools have become obscured in the controversy over the fact of difference. There have been those who have held that there is no difference whatever. This was the position taken by Paul T. Homan at the Round Table on Institutional Economics at the 1932 meeting of the American Economic Association. At the same meeting, R. T. Ely maintained that as far as he could determine, the institutionalists were not attempting to do anything that the young economists had not been trying at the time of the formation of the American Economic Association in the eighties. In fact, Ely held that ever since that time economists had been doing essentially what the institutionalists were claiming to have done.[1] These statements would indicate that there is no essential difference between the two schools, and this opinion is frequently found among recognized orthodox economists, who also cite various works of classical political economists as evidence to this effect.

A similar attitude is sometimes expressed with regard to institutional economics and the historical school of the nineteenth century. Since institutionalists are concerned with the evolution of behavior patterns from earlier forms, they do delve into the economic past of mankind. The historical school emphasized the necessity of gathering a large body of historical data from which general patterns could be discerned and generalizations drawn. Critics of the historical school have said that

---

[1] Paul T. Homan, "An Appraisal of Institutional Economics," *The American Economic Review,* XXII, No. 1, p. 17. See also comments of William W. Hewett and R. T. Ely, *ibid.,* pp. 105-116.

it failed to comprehend the interrelatedness of the empirical and the deductive approach. Since institutionalists are following the same procedure, they are chargeable with committing the same error. This is the position taken by Lewis Haney.[2]

Related to the notion that institutionalism emphasizes historicism is the claim that institutional economics emphasizes inductive technique while classical economics emphasizes deductive technique. Even some professed institutional economists lend credence to this belief. John Gambs, in a chapter on methodology in his little volume *Beyond Supply and Demand,* states that this distinction is "superficial" but nevertheless "has a rough elementary usefulness."[3] In line with this opinion, it is held that institutional economists advocate the gathering of "facts" about the present-day world; they are supposedly concerned with the photographic representation of the facts of the economic system as a going concern. Such interpreters point to empirical studies of labor, the business cycle, and the corporation as examples of institutional economics. This opinion is clearly expressed by A. G. Hart in the preface to his recent book on money.[4]

Some hold that institutional economics is concerned with the whole pattern of human activity, attempting to place the economic aspects of that behavior in relation to the larger whole of which economics is only a part. Adherents of this point of view claim that man's economic activity cannot be artificially separated from his other affairs; all of life is interrelated and separation into categories is an artificial device of the scholar which is apt to give a false impression of the life process. Economic affairs do not exist in a vacuum and economic activity is affected by all the rest of human activity. The institutionalist, it is held, differs from the classicist by recognition of this interrelatedness. Allan Gruchy, in a recent volume, holds that this difference in approach and viewpoint is the distinguishing mark of institutionalism. Classicists abstracted economic activity from the life process, giving a dis-

2 Lewis H. Haney, *op. cit.,* p. 748.

3 John Gambs, *op. cit.,* p. 54.

4 A. G. Hart, *Money, Debt, and Economic Activity,* New York, Prentice-Hall, 1948, p. vi.

torted picture of economic behavior, while institutional economists differ from the classicists "in their tendency to emphasize the importance of studying the economic system as a whole rather than as a collection of many unrelated parts."[5] He likens institutionalism to the "holistic" philosophy of Jan Smuts.

Still others have held that institutional economists emphasize the study of institutions. This idea is related to the last mentioned difference in that those who hold this view assume that the study of institutions is a broadening of economic inquiry from the narrow view of the classicist. It is assumed that the classicist ignored the fact that man is a creature whose behavior is molded by institutions. The classicist concerned himself with a free-wheeling man operating in accordance with free-will. The institutionalist studies institutions and focuses his attention on the effect of institutions on economic behavior.

John Gambs holds that the chief difference is the emphasis the institutionalist places on coercion. The classical economist, assuming that the economic universe was a harmonious one free from restraint and coercion, emphasized freedom of enterprise and individual self-help without interference. Gambs contends that the institutionalist views the economic universe as a coercive one in which coercion is brought to bear on those least able to protect themselves.[6]

From this cursory review it is obvious that there is no agreement on whether there is a difference, and neither is there agreement, if there is a difference, on just where that difference lies. To those such as Homan, who hold that there is no difference, it can be argued that classicists as well as institutionalists have made clear "aspects of problems, methods, and generalized knowledge" that differ significantly in institutionalism and classicism. Further, even a superficial examination of the work of some institutionalists, especially that of Veblen, would reveal a marked difference. Yet there seems to be no agreement among these men except that there is a difference.

Some of the differences that have been discussed, however, could better be called differences of emphasis rather than of

---

[5] Gruchy, *op. cit.*, p. viii.
[6] Gambs, *op. cit.*, p. 11.

degree. Classical economists have concerned themselves with the origin and development of the present economic system and many economists adhering to classical theory have engaged in gathering historical data. In fact, the largest proportion of work in economic history has been done by those of the classical faith, and at no time has the classicist denied the relevance of historical data. Adam Smith devoted a relatively large part of the *Wealth of Nations* to the historical background of capitalism.

The claim that classicism has been theoretical or deductive while institutionalism has been empirical or inductive is also invalid except with reference to degree. Not one of the classical economists has denied the value of the inductive method, and while it is true that classicism has built elaborate theoretical systems on a thin set of questionable assumptions, it should not be concluded from this that the classical economists dismiss induction as a method or that they make no use of induction. For that matter, the founders of classical political economy were of the opinion that the assumptions upon which they built their system were revealed to all by common sense, and did not require the drudgery of scholarly empirical verification. On the other hand, it is equally incorrect to hold that institutional economists make no use of deduction. There are, of course, so-called institutionalists who, despairing of the classical theory, have renounced theory *per se* and have engaged in multiplying facts for fact's sake. Certainly no one, however, would claim that the work of Veblen was not theoretical. The titles of his first two major works began with the word "Theory," as Veblen pointed out to H. J. Davenport when the latter accused him of neglecting theory.[7] If economic theory is defined as synonymous with the theoretical speculations of the classical economists, then there is of course no institutionalist theory, but this definition could be held seriously only by one very narrowly trained in classical theory. It would seem, then, that both classical and institutional economists adhere to deduction and induction.

The classical economist does not give much attention to the economic framework of his economic society because in all

[7] Joseph Dorfman, *op. cit.*, p. 311.

classical economics the institutional framework is taken for granted. As will be shown, the founders of classical political economy took the social organization of their time for granted as the product of a stable human nature characterized by common-sense reason. As the institutional economist has taken into consideration institutional patterns of behavior, it is assumed that he differs from classical political economy on this ground. But that is not quite the case, as there have been those whose study of the institutional structure is perfectly compatible with classical political economy. This is true of the work of Max Weber, who has been classified as an institutionalist by some, but who would better be classified as a student of economic sociology whose work is in no way incompatible with classical economics.[8] That the institutional economist has something more in mind than merely the influence of the institutional framework on a classically conceived human behavior is clear from the work of Veblen alone. Veblen not only delved into the institutional structure; he rejected classical political economy *in toto* and developed a "new economic theory." This rejection is clear in several of his early essays on methodology.[9] The idea that the institutionalist is one who studies institutions has also been rejected by present-day institutionalists. John Gambs has stated that institutional economics "is not institutional."[10] Unfortunately, the word institutionalism connotes the study of institutions and has come to designate this school of thought. C. E. Ayres, at the end of a long note in his *Theory of Economic Progress,* calls attention to the confusion engendered by this usage.

As a designation of a way of thinking in economics the term "institutionalism" is singularly unfortunate, since it points only at that from which an escape is being sought. Properly speaking, it is the

---

[8] Max Weber, *The Theory of Social and Economic Organization,* New York, Oxford, 1947. See the Introduction by Talcott Parsons, p. 31 and especially the long footnote on p. 40 in which Parsons severs all relationships between Weber and Veblen. This note should be studied carefullv by those who rather loosely throw Weber and Sombart in with the American institutionalists.

[9] Thorstein Veblen, *The Place of Science in Modern Civilization,* New York, Viking, 1942. See for instance "The Preconceptions of Economic Science," pp. 82-179.

[10] Gambs, *op. cit.,* p. 9.

classical tradition that is "institutionalism," since it is a way of thinking which expresses a certain set of institutions.[11]

To sum up, in view of the general confusion over the differences between these two schools of thought, it might well be asked if there is any marked difference. If there is no difference, then it would be better that all discussion cease, and the energy put into more constructive pursuits. On the other hand, if there is a marked difference, then the key to the difference remains to be found.

There is one possible way out of the confusion: an appeal to the institutionalists themselves. If there is some consensus among institutionalists on one point of difference between their work and that of traditional economics, therein may lie the key. In spite of apparently total confusion, there is one important point of difference that all institutional economists have stressed, even those who have favored some other difference as the major one: they all have criticized the classical political economists for failing to deal satisfactorily with change.

In one of his earliest essays Veblen claimed that the received economics was not an evolutionary one, and stated that, "from what has been said it appears that an evolutionary economics must be the theory of a process of cultural growth as determined by economic interest, a theory stated in terms of the process itself."[12] Veblen held that the traditional economists based their economic theory on a hedonistic psychology and accepted the natural-order preconceptions of the eighteenth century. The result was to develop a taxonomic science that was not in conformance with the trend of modern science to go beyond taxonomy to an explanation of the phenomena in terms of cumulative change and process. Economics in the hands of the classicists failed of the mark and their work was termed "pre-Darwinian."

Walton Hamilton called attention to the same dereliction on the part of classicists. Hamilton in an early paper claimed that the classical economists had "regarded social arrangements which had existed for the briefest moment in human history

---

11 C. E. Ayres, *The Theory of Economic Progress*, Chapel Hill, University of North Carolina Press, 1944, pp. 156-157n.

12 Veblen, *op. cit.*, p. 77.

as of the immutable cosmos itself." Nevertheless, man was beginning to view all phenomena as subject to change.[13] In a paper on institutional economics at the 1918 annual meeting of the American Economic Association, Hamilton held that the difference between institutionalism and classicism was "no pointless struggle in method to be carried on by breaking syllogisms over concepts and by engaging in polemics over niceties in statement." The disagreement "involves the very nature of the problems which the theorist should set himself; its real issue is over what economic theory is all about."[14] Hamilton held that an adequate economic theory should deal with cumulative change and that the traditional economics failed to meet the test of a valid theory by not dealing with change.

A decade later, in the *American Economic Review,* Morris A. Copeland likened economics to biology and held that it should be an evolutionary science. Economics was a social science and as such was not "primarily concerned with individual behavior." It was a biological science because "it studies group relationships among living organisms of the genus *homo sapiens."* As a biological and a social science economics must recognize the general meaning of biological evolution.[15]

John M. Clark has insisted that institutionalism is concerned with institutions, but deals with its data in terms of change.

> It takes for granted "retail" or piecemeal change as a continuous process, but it does not view such changes as did the typical nineteenth century liberal, who assumed that the essence of the institution (the stereotype) persisted unchanged by such piecemeal reforms of particular abuses. He views them rather as steps in the process of cumulative change or evolution.[16]

Although Willard E. Atkins claimed that institutionalists have points of disagreement and that what has been called institutional economics varies widely in character and scope, he

---

[13] Walton Hamilton, "The Development of Hoxie's Economics," *The Journal of Political Economy,* XXIV, No. 9, pp. 858-859.

[14] Walton Hamilton, "The Institutional Approach to Economic Theory," *American Economic Review,* IX, March 1919, pp. 309-318.

[15] Morris A. Copeland, "Economic Theory and the Natural Science Point of View," *American Economic Review,* XXI, No. 7, p. 68. See also opening statement in "Institutional Economics and Model Analysis" by Copeland in *American Economic Review,* XLI, No. 2, Supplement, p. 56.

[16] John Maurice Clark, Round Table Conference on Institutional Economics, *American Economic Review,* XXII, No. 1, Supplement, p. 105.

held that there were certain points of agreement among institutional economists. One of the points of agreement was that "economic behavior is constantly changing; therefore, economic generalizations should specify limits of culture and time to which they apply."[17]

All of these statements were made at least two decades ago. Within the last few years, however, at least four authors in four separate works on institutionalism have placed emphasis on change as being a distinguishing mark of institutional economics. Each has claimed that the classical economists failed to encompass change in their economic theory. Although he nowhere listed specifically the differences between institutional and classical economics, it is clear from *The Theory of Economic Progress* that C. E. Ayres holds classical economic theory to be essentially static and institutional theory to be dynamic. The difference between classical and institutional economics over change is implicit in his whole argument. Ceremonial behavior is essentially static in nature. The classical economist's focus of attention has been on price and the price system which is the essentially ceremonial aspect of contemporary culture. Classical theory has been static in consequence of the very phenomena which it chooses for analysis. Institutional theory, by giving instrumental behavior its proper place, is dynamic.[18]

Both Gambs and Gruchy have held that the major distinguishing mark of institutionalism is other than change. As was pointed out earlier, Gambs claims the major difference to be the institutionalist's acceptance of coercion as the dominant characteristic of economic behavior. Nevertheless, he also points out that the institutionalist gives an important place to change in his theory. Gambs suggests that the name "institutional" is not adequate and that Veblen would probably have chosen "evolutionary economics."[19] He holds that emphasis on evolutionary change is an important aspect of institutional economics that distinguishes it from the traditional brand.[20]

---

17 *Ibid.*, p. 111.
18 C. E. Ayres, *op. cit.* See especially Chaps. I-IV and VI-IX.
19 Gambs, *op. cit.*, p. 9.
20 *Ibid.*, p. 22 ff.

Although Allan Gruchy has claimed that the major difference is to be found in the "holistic"[21] approach of the institutionalist, he also stresses the importance of change. In fact it is difficult to differentiate between "holism" and evolutionary economics in Gruchy's discussion, as the following quotation well shows.

> Since no descriptive term which has been used by the economists, whose work is the center of interest in this study, has come into general acceptance, the term "holistic" has been adopted in this study to describe their economic thought. This term was coined by the eminent South African scholar and statesman, Jan Christian Smuts, from the Greek word *holos,* which means "whole." Smuts used the new term to describe the kind of scientific thinking which grew out of the researches of Charles Darwin (1859) in biological evolution, of Antoine Henri Becquerel (1895) in radioactivity, and of Albert Einstein (1915) in the theory of relativity. This type of economic thought is evolutionary or dynamic rather than mechanistic or static in its emphasis. It runs contrary to the type of thinking which dominated the pre-Darwinian world, and which provided the intellectual matrix from which came nineteenth century classical economic thought. The post-Darwinian type of economic thought which Smuts describes as "holistic" takes the physical world to be an evolving, dynamic whole or synthesis, which is not only greater than the sum of its parts, but which also so relates the parts that their functioning is conditioned by their interrelation.[22]

From the above passage it is clear that change is no less important in institutional economics than "holism." In fact Gruchy does not at any point treat "holism" as distinct from evolution and change. The use of the words "biological evolution," "evolutionary," "dynamic," "pre-Darwinian," "evolving," to describe and differentiate "holistic" from classical thought would indicate that emphasis on change is as important a difference as treating the economic process as a whole. At any rate, it is at least evident that Gruchy considers the treatment of change by institutionalists to be a distinguishing mark.

Although John R. Commons does not directly treat the problem of social change, his recent posthumous volume leaves no doubt that he considered economic behavior to be the product of evolution. He criticises what he calls the Newtonian outlook

---

[21] This was also stressed as a distinguishing mark by Gambs, *op. cit.*, p. 24 ff.
[22] Allan Gruchy, *op. cit.*, p. 4.

of the nineteenth-century economists,[23] and holds that economic action is collective action. This collective action is guided by what he calls working rules. Working rules are not something fixed and eternal, but are subject to change and development to meet the needs of a changing situation.[24] Institutions, which are a complex of working rules, are in a constant state of change and development, a product of continual readjustment to new needs.

It would seem to be a fair conclusion from all this testimony that institutional economists consider the concept of change to be an important distinguishing mark of institutional economics. Some have emphasized one difference as most important and some another, but the fact remains that all are agreed that institutionalism differs on this one question—change. The failure of all to agree on any other single difference would seem to indicate that change may be the key by which the difference between classical and institutional economics may be explained.

Classical political economy, of course, also claims to deal with change. At least since the time of Adam Smith classical political economy could not be said to have ignored change. In fact change, if not explicitly dealt with, is certainly implied in the economic system of Adam Smith. The nature of Smith's inquiry indicates that he assumed change, for his inquiry was concerned with the "nature and causes of the wealth of nations."

Moreover, all classical economists since the time of Smith have concerned themselves with change. As early as the time of John Stuart Mill the classical doctrine dealt with what was labeled economic dynamics. Later, John Bates Clark devoted a large part of his time to the development of dynamic economics.[25] This is no less true of some of the more recent work of classical economists. In fact, the concern over business cycles in recent years would indicate that the classical economist does recognize change at least to the extent that it is reflected in price changes and employment. Even without consideration of the

---

23 John R. Commons, *The Economics of Collective Action,* New York, Macmillan, 1951, p. 36.

24 *Ibid.*, pp. 23-35.

25 John Bates Clark, *The Distribution of Wealth,* New York, Macmillan, 1902, Chaps. XXV-XXVI, and *The Essentials of Economic Theory,* New York, Macmillan, 1915, Chap. XII ff.

business cycle, it could not be said that the classicist has neglected change.

Since a large body of classical doctrine purports to deal with change, how can it be said that the institutionalist differs from the classicist by taking change into his theory? In order to answer this question, it must be shown that the difference between the two schools of thought lies (1) in the concept of change, or, (2) in disagreement over what changes, or, (3) both of these.

It will be shown in this inquiry that the difference between the two lies in the concept both of the nature of change and of what changes. The classicist has always viewed change as discontinuous and has held that it is a re-establishment of an equilibrium or state of quiescence. The cause of change is independent of the economy; change is caused by disturbing elements from without the system. A new adjustment must be made in response to the disturbance caused by these elements.

The institutionalist, on the other hand, considers change to be a part of the economic process. Instead of viewing the economy as a fixed system periodically prodded into movement to a new point of non-motion, he holds that the economy is at all times undergoing a process of cumulative change, and that, the study of economics is the study of process.

II

NEWTONIANISM AND DARWINISM IN ECONOMIC THEORY

If it can be shown that classical economics has assumed a theory of change peculiar to one time and place and institutional economics has assumed a theory of change peculiar to another time and place, it should then be possible to show how these assumptions have affected the theoretical structures of the two schools and thereby bring out clearly their differences.

Both Newtonianism and Darwinism had profound and far-reaching effects on the habits of thought of mankind. Both affected man's concept of change, not only of change in the physical universe, but of change in the social universe as well. Developments in one area of human inquiry frequently complement developments in other areas, but in addition to being complementary, frequently the advance in one area may be of such an epochal nature that it colors the habits of thought of mankind in many other areas of inquiry. Certainly this could be said of the work both of Newton and of Darwin. The eighteenth century has frequently been called the "Age of Newton." Newton interpreted the physical universe in terms of natural law. The social philosophers of the eighteenth century borrowed his technique of explanation to analyze the social structure of their time. Several writers, including Carl Becker, have called attention to the fact that the eighteenth century was the Newtonian century just as the nineteenth was the Darwinian and the twentieth that of Einstein. Everyone talked of Newton whether he had read the *Principia* or not. As one writer has stated the case,

Newton's great mathematical system of the world struck the imagination of the educated class of his time and spread with amazing swiftness, completing what Descartes had begun. Prior to 1789 some eighteen editions of the difficult and technical *Principia* were called for; British universities were teaching it by the end of the seventeenth century, and Newton was accorded a royal funeral when he died in 1727. In 1734, Bernouli won the prize of the French Academy of Science with a Newtonian memoir; in 1740 the last prize was granted to an upholder of Descartes' physics. Voltaire was struck by Newtonianism during his visit to England in 1726-1728, and popularized him in France in his *English Letters,* in 1734, and his *Elements of the Newtonian Philosophy* in 1738; thenceforth Newton reigned in France as in England. From the presses there poured forth an immense stream of popular accounts for those unable or unwilling to pursue the classic work. His conclusions and his picture of the world were accepted on authority. By 1789 there had appeared about the *Principia* forty books in English, seventeen in French, three in German, eleven in Latin, one in Portuguese, and one in Italian, many of them like those of Decaguilers, Benjamin Martin, Ferguson's *Lectures for Ladies and Gentlemen,* and Count Alogrotti's *Le Newtonianisme pour les Dames,* running through edition after edition. Newton's name became a symbol which called up the picture of the scientific machine-universe, the last word in science, one of those uncriticized preconceptions which largely determined the social and political and religious as well as the strictly scientific thinking of the age. Newton was science, science was the eighteenth century ideal.[1]

Newtonianism rapidly spread to every area of human inquiry. It was eagerly seized upon by the social philosophers, purportedly as a means of analyzing social phenomena in the same manner and light that Newton had analyzed the physical universe. The "method of the new physical science became all important, for men proceeded to apply it in every field of investigation."[2] The social sciences in the Age of Enlightenment were "almost completely under the domination of the physiomathematical method,"[3] and the "two leading ideas of the eighteenth century, Nature and Reason, . . . derived their meaning from the natural sciences, and carried over to man, led to the attempt to discover a social physics."[4]

The eighteenth century viewed social forms as fixed in nature and what change took place was at most a quantitative one within fixed limits set by a natural order of things. The universe was a mechanical piece often likened to a clock whose moving parts, when once wound up by a divine Creator, would run eternally in the same pre-established mechanical arrangement.[5] The best interest of man could be attained by an objective scrutiny of the workings of this mechanical universe. This inquiry

1 John H. Randall, Jr., *The Making of the Modern Mind,* Boston, Houghton-Mifflin, 1926, p. 260.

2 *Ibid.,* p. 261.

3 *Ibid.*

4 *Ibid.,* p. 225.

5 *Ibid.,* p. 275.

was to be guided by reason, which would uncover the great principles by which the social universe was guided in its rhythmical pattern of movement. By laying bare these principles man would be able to conform to them and thus would enhance his contentment and happiness on earth. Misery and despair, the product of man's ignorance, which was also the source of his folly in flaunting these immutable natural principles, could be banished from the world. It was indeed a century of optimism. This optimism was not limited to the way in which man viewed the physical universe. In the area of social inquiry as well, man could by his own reason put his finger on the heart of the social universe.

Eighteenth-century social thought was like that of the Renaissance in that the classical civilizations were viewed as a golden past that had become contaminated by the church fathers of the medieval period.[6] However, one significant difference separated the thought of these two periods. Whereas the thinkers of the Renaissance felt that man's salvation rested in a return to and reverence for the classical civilization, the men of the eighteenth century held that man's salvation rested in an enlightened reason. Reason would reveal the workings of the natural universe and assure man of a civilization more than matching that of classical times at their best.

Although some writers have correctly pointed out the revolutionary effects of the displacement of the medieval cosmology by the new way of viewing things,[7] eighteenth-century social thought was not as revolutionary as some of its chief progenitors and many of its later interpreters held it to be. It represented a point of view that had its roots in the past and its branches in what has become the present, linking the view of the churchmen and the contemporary view. The whole point of Carl Becker's book is to show this relationship. As he states,

> My object is, therefore, to furnish an explanation of eighteenth century thought, from the historical view, by showing that it was related to something that came before and to something else that came after.[8]

[6] Carl Becker, *The Heavenly City of the Eighteenth Century Philosophers,* New Haven; Yale University Press, 1932, pp. 115-118.

[7] Harold J. Laski, *The Rise of European Liberalism,* London, George Allen and Unwin, 1947, p. 72.

[8] Becker, *op. cit.,* p. 29.

For God, the eighteenth-century philosophers substituted Nature. Again, as Becker so well points out,

> . . . the disciples of the Newtonian philosophy had not ceased to worship. They had only given another form and a new name to the object of worship: having denatured God, they deified nature. They could therefore, without self-consciousness, and with only a slight emendation in the sacred text repeat the cry of the psalmist: "I will lift up mine eyes to Nature from whence cometh my help!"[9]

This of course is not to depreciate the importance of the change. Although Nature may have replaced God, Nature was not sanctified by Holy Writ; and the divine rule of Nature was not one that was beyond the question of mere mortals.

The universe created by the handiwork of a beneficent Nature, however, was as eternal and fixed as that which had been created, by proxy, by the medieval agents of the divine Creator. It was, in addition, a revealed order of things, revealed not by divine agents, but by the reasonable work of Nature herself. To be able to see this point was to be truly enlightened.[10] "Nature was thought through and through orderly and rational; hence what was natural was easily identified with what was rational, and conversely, whatever particularly in human society, seemed to an intelligent man reasonable, was regarded as natural, as somehow rooted in the very nature of things."[11] Within this frame of thought it was possible to establish a well-ordered life, for a well-ordered life was one that was natural, and what was natural would be revealed to reasonable men by the exercise of reason. Only slothfulness in the exercise of this natural power had allowed man to become a slave to unnatural institutions that had made of life a miserable thing at best.

But what is of major significance in the doctrine of the eighteenth-century philosophers is the full acceptance of Newtonian mechanics as adequate for analysis of the social universe. To the men of the eighteenth century the social universe, like the heavens, was made up of individually suspended bodies, an orderly relationship among them being assured by natural forces. For Newton's law of gravitation the eighteenth-century social philosopher used "self-interest." Each individual by exer-

---

[9] *Ibid.*, p. 63.
[10] *Ibid.*, pp. 50-51.
[11] Randall, *op. cit.*, p. 276.

cising his "natural right" to seek his own self-interest untrammeled by disturbing elements would simply be promoting the social good as well as his own welfare. Since each free-wheeling individual was seeking his own self-interest, it was impossible for any of these individually suspended bodies to crash—for it was to the self-interest of each to avoid such a crash. Thus self-interest acted both as a compelling and a repelling force just as Newton's gravitational pull and laws of motion balanced off one another so that heavenly spheres moved around one another in an elliptical pattern.

The constants in the system of the social philosophers were human nature and the social structure of their time. Movement among individuals took place within a fixed social framework in accordance with self-interest. Since they assumed that man was endowed by Nature with Reason and believed that they themselves were living in an enlightened era, it was not difficult to make the further assumption that the social order of their day was the natural product of sufficient reason and therefore fixed. "Natural liberty" was the concern of all and natural liberty meant to all a society in which self-interest was the only organizational force.

But what has all this to do with economic theory? Why delve into the past? Is not contemporary orthodox theory free of any "natural-order" preconceptions? After all, "equilibrium is just equilibrium." But classical political economy is a product of the eighteenth-century habits of thought, and this is no less true of the "dynamic economics" of a Kenneth Boulding or a J. R. Hicks than it was of the economics of Adam Smith. In fact it is revealing to see the full acceptance of Newtonian change by Adam Smith, for contemporary classical political economy has antecedents no matter how vehemently it may deny this past and despite any mental gymnastics that may be attempted to the same end.

The whole basis of modern price theory is to be found in Adam Smith without the "modern refinements." The world of Adam Smith was a Newtonian one and like his contemporary philosophers he accepted the social order of his day as a naturally self-equilibrating one. In his price theory he shows in an unadulterated form the Newtonian scheme of thought turned to the analysis of social phenomena. According to Smith, "There is in every society or neighborhood an ordinary or average rate of wages and profit" and "This rate is naturally regulated."[12] There is in addition a natural rate of rent. "When the price of any commodity is neither more nor less than what is sufficient to pay the rent of the land, the wages of the labour, and the profits of the stock employed in raising, preparing, and bringing it to market, according to their natural rates, the commodity is then sold for what may be called its natural price."[13] The price at which a commodity actually sells is known as the market price. This market price has a tendency to "gravitate" around the natural price, but it is always being turned back toward the natural price by the force of self-interest as manifested in supply and demand. According to Smith, effective demand is made up of all those "who are willing to pay the natural price of the commodity."[14] Should the quantity brought to market be less than effective demand, the self-interest of some would lead them to bid a little more than the natural price for the commodity. This bidding would cause the price to move above the natural price, resulting in a surplus in the form of profit. The profit would attract additional quantities of the commodity to be offered, the effect of which would be to turn the market price back toward the natural price. In case the supply exceeded effective demand, some producers would be tempted to take a little less for their commodity rather than be without sales. This would force a reduction in the market price below the natural price. Some of the component parts of the natural price would receive less than their natural rate and would withdraw from participation in the production of the commodity. This would force a decrease in supply and would force the market price back toward the natural price.[15] In an unmistakably Newtonian passage Adam Smith summarizes these movements as follows:

> The natural price, therefore, is, as it were, the central price, to which the prices of all commodities are continually gravitating. Different accidents may sometimes keep them suspended a good

[12] Adam Smith, *The Wealth of Nations*, New York, Modern Library, 1937, p. 55.
[13] *Ibid.*
[14] *Ibid.*, p. 56.
[15] *Ibid.*, pp. 56 ff.

deal above it, and sometimes force them down even somewhat below it. But whatever may be the obstacles which hinder them from settling in this center of repose and continuance, they are constantly tending towards it.[16]

Although this explanation of competitive price has become more sophisticated with one hundred and seventy-five years of refinement, it is still essentially the accepted explanation of competitive price.[17] At no point in economic theory is the influence of the Newtonian concept of change more clearly shown than in the usual analysis of competitive price. Prices are seen as "gravitating" about a norm or natural point, always being repelled from this point, but also always being forced back toward it by the "pull" of self-interest. The price system works, it moves resources in accordance with natural forces. And price when explained in this fashion is a Newtonian mechanism. The very fact that classical political economy views price as a system is evidence that its outlook on price is essentially Newtonian.

Since the time of Smith, change has meant, to the classical economist, a quantitative change in output induced by a quantitative change in price. Despite later innovations and sophistications, this is no less true of contemporary classical economic theory than it was of that of Adam Smith. Anyone in doubt need only peruse the elementary texts provided in great quantity by the contemporary classical economists. The mechanics of Adam Smith have been modified by the injection of monopolistic and imperfect competition. But this, too, is cut in the same mechanical Newtonian pattern, the only significant change being that of the slope of the average revenue curve. Certainly the preconceptions underlying modern price theory as amended by monopolistic competition are the same.

In sum, the orthodox political economy which came out of the eighteenth century was Newtonian in outlook. It has ever since borne the Newtonian stamp, and this is especially true in its acceptance of the Newtonian mechanical concept of change. This was true of the earliest formal presentation of an elaborate body of economic doctrine by Adam Smith. It is no less true of the present-day classical economics.

16 *Ibid.*, p. 58.

17 Kenneth E. Boulding, *Economic Analysis*, New York, Harper, 1948, Chaps. 5, 7.

Institutionalism is a product of the Darwinian climate of opinion of the late nineteenth century. Darwinism has colored twentieth-century social thought just as Newtonianism colored eighteenth-century social thought, and the difference between institutionalism and the traditional economics can be largely explained by this difference in climate of opinion. Darwinism represented a revolution in habits of thought. The whole way of thought characterized by the natural-order preconceptions was gone, as evolution, conceived as an endless process of cumulative change, replaced the old static view of things. Whereas formerly social structure had been conceived by the Newtonians as something fixed in the natural universe, those influenced by the Darwinian revolution saw social structure as something arrived at through a process of cumulative change and as something undergoing further change.

Of course not everyone interpreted Darwin in this fashion. There were some like William Graham Sumner who saw in Darwin proof of the compulsive nature of competition working through the free market. The natural order stemming from the Newtonian concepts was thus made compatible with Darwinism. But this interpretation of Darwin mistook the process of natural selection for the whole Darwinian concept of evolutionary change; and it was the broader interpretation that was to influence the newer social thought of the age.[18]

Institutionalism was subject to this influence. No one saw the significance of the Darwinian revolution on social thought more clearly than did Veblen. Professor Hofstadter has called attention to this as follows:

> While other economists had found in Darwinian science merely a source of plausible analogies or a fresh rhetoric to substantiate traditional postulates and precepts, Veblen saw it as a model by which the whole fabric of economic thinking must be rewoven. The prevailing line of thought had said that the existing is the normal and the normal is the right, and that the roots of human ills lie in acts which interfere with the natural unfolding of this normal process toward its inherent end in a beneficent order. In so far as economists had taken hold of Darwinism, it was only to fortify this theoretical structure. Henceforth economics was to abandon such pre-

---

[18] Richard Hofstadter, *Social Darwinism in American Thought*, Philadelphia, University of Pennsylvania Press, 1944, Chaps. VII, VIII.

conceived notions and devote itself to a theory of the evolution of institutions as they are.[19]

The fact that institutionalism represents a revolutionary view in economics, and does so chiefly because of the Darwinian revolution, may explain its evolutionary nature; but it does not explain the fact that this was "an American movement to reconstruct economic science," "the most distinctive American contribution to the progress of economic science."[20] In particular, the fact that institutionalism broke out in America remains unexplained. The Darwinian revolution had affected the thought of all western civilization, yet it was in America that economic thought was reworked in terms of the full meaning of Darwinism.

That fact can be explained at least partially by a look at the American scene at the time of the outbreak of the "new economics." In the late nineteenth century the industrial revolution, which had already shaken Britain and British thought in the first half of the nineteenth century had begun to transform America. This was a period of rapid advance in science and of rapid expansion of an industrial technology that was transforming the living habits of a continent. Each day saw the birth of a new industry and the relegation of the old to the industrial scrap heap. A new continent was also creating a new society. The heavy hand of the past was not quite as heavy on the New World as on the Old, and the habits of thought peculiar to a different time and place were daily subject to question. Many of the old patterns of thought were found irrelevant and in the nature of excess baggage.

The influence of this climate of opinion on the rise of institutionalism has been well put by Walton Hamilton in an account of the economics of R. F. Hoxie.

> The third of these larger influences was the natural environment. The uncertainty which we have just detected alike in economic theory and in intellectual attitude was in large measure a result of the accelerated development of the industrial system. Peculiarly enough, the England of classical theory and the Germany of the historical school have left no conscious mark on Hoxie's work. His

19 *Ibid.*, pp. 132-133.
20 Allan Gruchy, *Modern Economic Thought*, p. vii.

material environment was that of contemporary America. A continent, possessed of unparalleled resources, had just been subjugated by the aid of the machine process. An aggregation of trades, processes, and markets was being forged into an industrial system. Through a network of institutions, themselves in process of being created, these were coming to be a delicately balanced pecuniary system. On industrial lines, and impelled by the machine culture, society was being resolved into classes, smaller ones, each conscious of its inalienable right to large pecuniary income. Individuals were beginning to become conscious of their group interest, the while they saw a threat in the assertion of the group interests of others. Change was everywhere. Wealth was increasing; accumulated capital was being invested and new capital values were emerging without investment; old industries were being expanded and new ones were springing up; the advance of technology was making obsolete productive processes which a moment before were new; and population was increasing to meet new pecuniary demands, bringing a babel of tongues and a motley culture.

Changes such as these defied expression in quantitative terms. The adjective "normal" seemed strangely inappropriate when applied to any aspect of the situation; in the perpetual newness of things all must be "natural" or all unnatural. Nor could the situation be expressed in static terms. It offered no disposition to return to an "equilibrium" after a "disturbing force" had disarranged the gear. It might well be that a series of actions and reactions was tending toward such a consummation; but if so, they were of negligible importance, for they could not stem the onward tide of the highly dynamic forces which were drawing industrial society into an unknown future. In fact, the whole system was so new that little could be known of the real forces at work; but amid the unknown, the mark of reality seemed much more legible in tendency than in existing fact. The less important "being" was swallowed up in the more important "becoming." First static theory, and later the quantitative "dynamics" which was added to it, seemed foreign to the contemporary American of perpetual transition.[21]

In this type of environment an evolutionary economics of post-Darwinian character could spawn and grow. Thus, it was on the American economic front that institutional economics developed.

Although it can be shown that both classical and institutional economic theory deal with change, it can be just as clearly shown that their concepts of change differ. One is Newtonian, seeing change as a quantitative and repetitive movement within

[21] Walton Hamilton, "The Development of Hoxie's Economics," pp. 859-860.

a fixed universe. In the Newtonian scheme, a divine Maker has been replaced by Nature, but as Carl Becker has pointed out there is a marked resemblance between the divine Maker and Nature.[22] Veblen holds that the Newtonian outlook as manifested in the social thought of the eighteenth-century philosophers is animistic. Nature is viewed as a careful and clever craftsman who has constructed a mechanical universe to run in perpetuity. All of the work of nature and thus all of the movements of the social universe are viewed as directed to some right and good end. In this sense it is teleological.[23] Although the Newtonian concept of change is more matter-of-fact than that of preceding concepts, it is essentially animistic and teleological.

Darwinian change, on the other hand, is a non-teleological process of cumulative growth. There is no right and good end toward which things are working out. This difference separates the classical economic theory from institutional theory, affecting every aspect of theory of each school of thought. The effect of these different conceptions of change on classical and institutional economic theory can be shown by an examination of the psychology underlying the two types of doctrine, by an analysis of the concepts of social organization, and by a comparison of the theories of economic progress. We will inquire into each of these in turn in the next three chapters.

---

22 Becker, *op. cit.*, p. 63.

23 Veblen, *The Place of Science in Modern Civilization*, pp. 88-89.

III

CHANGE AND HUMAN NATURE

Classical economics rests upon hedonistic preconceptions. But hedonism has been discredited as a valid psychology. Therefore, it is now the tendency of the contemporary classical economist to deny his hedonistic preconceptions or even to deny the relevancy of psychology to economics. This denial is the result of a gradual process. In fact, the retreat of orthodox political economists from repeated criticisms of their basic psychological propositions can be compared to the disorganized but repeated retreat of the World War II Allies to "previously prepared positions" in the early years of the late war. At one time the classicists stood firm against all attacks on hedonism.[1] But, worsted in the struggle, they retreated from pleasure and pain to utility and disutility in the belief that this new position was successfully camouflaged.[2] This new defense was soon uncovered, and the orthodox theorist retreated to a new position called "indifference."[3] At the present time he has resorted to a denial of the necessity of fighting over psychology and even of the necessity of building an economic theory on adequate and modern psychological conceptions.

Thus Professor Robbins holds that psychology is addicted to fads and that it is impossible for the economist to rewrite his theory in conformance with the fickle notions of psychologists. The economist, he thinks, must proceed on psychological premises that are beyond scientific verification by the psychologist, i.e., common sense. This is the only meaning that can be attributed to the following passage:

> It is sometimes thought, even at the present day, that this notion of relative valuation depends upon the validity of particular psychological doctrine. The borderlands of Economics are the happy hunting-ground of minds averse to the effort of exact thought, and, in these ambiguous regions, in recent years, endless time has been devoted to attacks on the alleged psychological assumptions of Eco-

[1] W. S. Jevons, *Theory of Political Economy,* London, Macmillan, 1888, Chaps. II, III.

[2] Alfred Marshall, *Principles of Economics,* London, Macmillan, 1930, pp. 140-141.

[3] Hicks, *Value and Capital,* Oxford, Oxford University Press, 1946, pp. 2 ff.

nomic Science. Psychology, it is said, advances very rapidly. If, therefore, Economics rests upon particular psychological doctrines, there is no task more ready to hand than every five years or so to write sharp polemics showing that, since psychology has changed its fashion, Economics needs "rewriting from the foundation upwards." As might be expected, the opportunity has not been neglected. Professional economists, absorbed in the exciting task of discovering new truth, have usually disclaimed to reply: and the lay public, ever anxious to escape the necessity of recognizing the implications of choice in a world of scarcity, has allowed itself to be bamboozled into believing that matters, which are in fact as little dependent on the truth of fashionable psychology as the multiplication table, are still open questions on which the enlightened man, who, of course, is nothing if not a psychologist, must be willing to suspend judgment.[4]

In answer to Professor Robbins it might be pointed out that the concept of a schedule of preferences alluded to in the above passage and discussed at greater length in other parts of the volume is not something verifiable by common sense. This concept comes from the Benthamite hedonic calculus. In fact, to the extent that this postulate remains a key prop to the theoretical expostulations of the classical school, it lends a hedonistic color to their entire economic theory. The classical economist is in no danger from the fads of psychology. He has not even kept up with the verified and valid advance of psychological knowledge.

This is a misfortune. For despite the "polemics" of Professor Robbins, economics has always had a close relation to psychology. Frequently its psychological preconceptions have been implied rather than explicit. Since economics purports to be a science of human behavior even in its most sterile price speculations, it always makes implicit assumptions as to the nature of man and human behavior.

As testimony to the truth of this statement, even a limited examination of economic doctrine from the time of the classical formulators down to the present reformulators reveals a rather consistent concept of human nature. To the early classicists, man was a self-seeking creature with a careful eye for taking full advantage of the main chance. Adam Smith's economic man was a shrewd calculator of pecuniary advantage. Through-

[4] Lionel Robbins, *The Nature and Significance of Economic Science,* London, Macmillan, 1935, pp. 83-84.

out Smith's economics that assumption as to the character of human nature is implicit. The human species is endowed with a natural instinct to "truck, barter, and exchange one thing for another." Society is simply a reflection of this tendency of original human nature.

This calculating and reasoning aspect of human nature is evident in that "early and rude state" that must have preceded western European civilization. Primitive man was a being uncontaminated by institutions of property and ownership, and therefore he was free to exercise his pure reason. But he was also a creature of sensations, feeling the pain of effort or the irksomeness of labor. Says Smith:

> In that early and rude state of society which precedes both the accumulation of stock and the appropriation of land, the proportion between the quantities of labour necessary for acquiring different objects seems to be the only circumstances which can afford any rule for exchanging them for another. If among a nation of hunters, for example, it usually costs twice the labour to kill a beaver which it does to kill a deer, one beaver should naturally exchange for or be worth two deer. It is natural that what is usually the produce of two day's or two hour's labour, should be worth double of what is usually the purchase of one day's or one hour's labour.[5]

Reasonable man would naturally take thought, weighing hedonistically the relative labor cost of procuring a beaver as against a deer, and would arrive at a reasonable answer based on the proportions of irksomeness and cunning in capturing each.

The whole classical analysis of supply is in hedonic terms. Goods, the product of pain and exertion, exchange for goods produced by equivalent pain and exertion. No other meaning can be attributed to the labor theory of value. As Adam Smith states the case, labor is irksome and the laborer in exerting himself "must always lay down the same portion of his ease, his liberty, and his happiness."[6] In this sentence is evidence of an acceptance of hedonism. Labor is painful and is undertaken at the cost of happiness. Again he states "The real price of every thing, what every thing really costs to the man who wants to acquire it, is the toil and trouble of acquiring it."[7]

It is true that Adam Smith abandoned the strict labor

---

[5] Smith, *op. cit.*, p. 47.
[6] *Ibid.*, p. 33.
[7] *Ibid.*, p. 30.

quantity theory in society once removed from the "early and rude stage." Once the landlord and capitalist arrive on the scene and engross a part of the annual produce of labor, Smith resorts to a cost of production theory. Ricardo, however, takes Adam Smith to task for abandoning the labor theory of value in this more advanced state of society.[8] Ricardo holds that commodities derive their value from the quantity of labor involved in their production at any stage in society. He quotes with approval the hedonic passages just referred to in Adam Smith,[9] demonstrating that he too accepted a hedonic explanation of value. This holds for all commodities with the exception of those non-reproducible commodities "the value of which is determined by their scarcity alone."[10] But these items are few in number and do not invalidate the labor theory of value as a general theory.[11]

In the hands of the classical economists, value was deter-

---

[8] David Ricardo, *The Principles of Political Economy and Taxation,* London, J. M. Dent, 1937, Everyman's Edition, pp. 7-9.

[9] *Ibid.*, pp. 6-7.

[10] *Ibid.*, p. 6.

[11] This is the prevailing interpretation of Ricardo's value theory; but Professor E. E. Hale of the University of Texas, interprets Ricardo somewhat differently, holding that Ricardo thought of labor as the *measure* of value but not as its *source.* See also Jacob H. Hollander, "The Development of Ricardo's Theory of Value," *Quarterly Journal of Economics,* August, 1904. Perhaps, as Eric Roll suggests, Ricardo was somewhat confused. "Ricardo uncovers the confusion in Smith's statement of the theory. . . . But Ricardo is not free from confusion himself. He says that the determination of this relative value of commodities helps to determine how changes in the ratio in which commodities exchange arise, and speaks in another place also of the comparative values of commodities. However, relative value, as he calls it, may change equally for two commodities if the amount of labor necessary to produce them alters at the same rate, thus leaving their comparative value (the ratio of exchange) unchanged. Ricardo seems to be unaware of this double meaning. He claims that his interest is in the variations in the relative value of commodities and not in their absolute (or real) value. Yet it is clear that his own labor theory of value refers precisely to that absolute value. It is this confusion between (labor-determined) value and the ratio of exchange which was later to be used by Bailey in his attack on Ricardo. Ricardo tries to show that labor creates value in capitalist as well as in primitive conditions of production. In section 3 of the first chapter, he states that not only present but past labor, embodied in implements, tools, buildings, and the like, determines value. The equipment which is used in production represents so much stored-up labor which enters into the value of the product as it is used up. The question of ownership (that is, of the particular social conditions of production) does not affect the result. Value remains determined by current and stored-up labor, whether the latter belongs to the laborer or not." Eric Roll, *A History of Economic Thought,* pp. 188-189. The present discussion is of course concerned only with the psychological assumptions of the labor theory, not with its distributive consequences.

mined by the quantity of labor necessary to the production or reproduction of a commodity. The implicit psychological assumption underlying the theory is that work or productive effort is irksome or painful. The corollary following from this, although not explicitly stated, is that consumption is pleasant. Thus, work or pain is undertaken in order to satisfy some pleasant end, or consumption. Even though the classicists went no further than an explanation of supply based on the irksomeness of labor, they were hedonistic. Pain is explicitly accepted as a force to be encountered in human nature; pleasure as a force is implied. Rational and calculating men will exchange commodities in the general course of events only for other commodities representing an equivalent in pain.

But there is more than this to identify classical political economy with the hedonistic psychology. As Elie Halevy has demonstrated in his remarkable volume, *The Growth of Philosophic Radicalism,* there was a close identity between the Utilitarians and the later classical economists.[12] In fact, James Mill devoted a great deal of his effort to the propagation of the work of both Ricardo and Bentham. Both assumed an identity of interests among men. In the case of the strict Benthamites this identity of interest was assured through the law of sympathy. According to the classical economists, the identity of interests was assured through the working of natural law. Hedonism was accepted as a matter of common sense and did not require any scientific verification. As a consequence, classical political economy had hedonistic preconceptions imbedded in it through the labor theory of value.

But the labor theory of value led to difficulties and to a seemingly new psychology. In Ricardian economic theory, the receipt of profit was left without a hedonistic justification.[13] Adam Smith had held that in the more advanced state of society in which ownership and property had developed, "the whole produce of labour does not always belong to the labourer."[14] The capitalist and the landlord appropriate for themselves a

12 Elie Halevy, *The Growth of Philosophic Radicalism,* London, Faber and Faber, 1949, Part I, Chap. III; Part II, Chap. II, Chap. III, pp. 251-282; Part III, Chap. I.

13 Ricardo, *op. cit.,* Chap. VI.

14 Smith, *op. cit.,* p. 49.

part of this surplus. Senior therefore attempted to place the same justification on profits as on wages by claiming that capital was accumulated through undergoing the "pain of abstinence." Thus, interest was paid in amount just sufficient to overcome the reluctance to save because of the painfulness of saving. On these grounds the capitalist was held to be paid for undergoing a special kind of pain, the pain of abstinence.

But this attempt by Senior to justify profit was not strong enough to offset the Ricardian socialists and the later conclusions of Marx.[15] As a consequence, later classical political economy dropped the labor theory of value. But what is of importance to the present discussion is the fact that hedonism was not dropped with it. Although the shift in the basis of value from pain to pleasure is generally considered not to have been accomplished until after the work of John Stuart Mill, there is evidence of what was to come in the work of Mill. He is supposed to have been only a synthesizer of classical political economy, yet he represents a transitional phase in the development of classical theory. Mill stated that "Happily, there is nothing in the laws of value which remains for the present or any future writer to clear up,"[16] but his own analysis of value foreshadows later subjective theory. In fact, there is evidence of the Marshallian synthesis in the following:

> That a thing may have any value in exchange, two conditions are necessary. It must be of some use; that is (as already explained), it must conduce to some purpose, satisfy some desire. No one will pay a price, or part with anything which serves some of his purposes, to obtain a thing which serves none of them. But, secondly, the thing must not only have some utility, there must also be some difficulty in its attainment.[17]

Although Mill may seem to be merely reiterating the position of Smith and Ricardo, such is not exactly the case. Smith and Ricardo talked about value in use, citing only the physical fact of use.[18] In Mill the word "use" means that the object used must "satisfy some desire." This is closely related to subjective value and it is an easy move to the subjective theory of value

[15] Werner Stark, *The Ideal Foundations of Economic Thought,* New York, Oxford University Press, 1944, pp. 51-148.

[16] J. S. Mill, *Principles of Political Economy,* London, Longmans, Green, 1909, p. 436.

[17] *Ibid.,* p. 442.

[18] Smith, *op. cit.,* p. 28; Ricardo, *op. cit.,* p. 5.

once the labor theory of value is out of the way. It was a result of the rise of the Ricardian socialists, the injection of Marxism, and the influence of utilitarianism in classical political economy that the shift was made from pain to pleasure as a basis of value.

Although not the first to formulate the new subjective value theory, Böhm-Bawerk was one of the early formulators who clearly demonstrates the fact that its significance as an offset to the Marxian position was well understood. Böhm-Bawerk devoted one whole book to an attempt to destroy the Marxian labor theory of value. That he understood its importance is made clear from the first chapter.

> The pillars of the system of Marx are his conception of value and his law of value. Without them, as Marx repeatedly asserts, all scientific knowledge of economic facts would be impossible.[19]

The rapidity of acceptance of the new subjective theory of value may thus have been more than deference for the logical consistency of the new doctrine. For by taking the basis of value away from labor, it was possible to eliminate the conclusions of the Marxians. Because Böhm-Bawerk's efforts were obviously directed to this end, and because of the clear utilitarianism of his definition of subjective value, his formulation of the marginal-utility theory is of especial interest here.

As formulated by Böhm-Bawerk the new theory revealed its utilitarian background. He distinguished value "in the Subjective and value in the Objective sense," and held that subjective value "is the importance which a good, or a complex of goods, possesses with regard to the well-being of a subject," while objective value is "the Power or Capacity of a good to procure some one objective result."[20] The latter is similar in meaning to contemporary instrumental value theory, but is not as broad in scope. The relationship between utilitarianism and subjective value is made clear in a further elaboration by Böhm-Bawerk:

> In this sense I should say of any particular good that it was valuable to me, if I recognized that my well being was so associated with it that the possession of it satisfied some want, secured me a gratifica-

---

[19] Eugen von Böhm-Bawerk, *Karl Marx and the Close of His System,* New York, Augustus Kelly, 1949, p. 9.

[20] Eugen von Böhm-Bawerk, *The Positive Theory of Capital,* New York, G. E. Stechert and Co., n. d., p. 130.

tion or a feeling of pleasure which I should not have had without it, or saved me from a pain which, otherwise, I should have had to endure.[21]

In this statement Böhm-Bawerk's relationship to utilitarianism is quite clear even to the use of the words, pleasure and pain. It is with subjective value that the economist has to do, objective value being relegated largely to the physical scientist and the engineer.[22]

According to Böhm-Bawerk, "All goods without exception . . . possess a certain relation to human well being."[23] However, this relation is not in all cases of an equally high grade. Goods may have a capacity to contribute to human well-being, and goods that do this belong to the lower grade. On the other hand, goods may be an essential "condition of human well being—a condition of such a kind that some gratification stands or falls with the having or wanting of the good."[24] In everyday life these grades of value have come to acquire the titles usefulness and value, the latter being the term for the higher grade. Thus, it becomes clear that relative scarcity is essential in order that goods may have value. If a good is so scarce that some wants which it could satisfy must go unsatisfied, the good has value.

Böhm-Bawerk claims that this view of value solves the old paradox that plagued classical political economists. To them it was a strange fact that goods such as iron with a high use value had a low exchange value, while on the other hand, goods such as diamonds with a low use value had a high exchange value. This problem was never satisfactorily solved and "innumerable theorists . . . have fallen back upon quite foreign and often wonderful lines of explanation, such as labour or labour time."[25]

The error of these early economists is found in the fact that they considered wants only from the standpoint of kinds of wants. But everyone has a scale for kinds of wants, ranked

---

21 *Ibid.*, p. 130.
22 *Ibid.*, p. 131.
23 *Ibid.*, p. 133.
24 *Ibid.*
25 *Ibid.*, p. 139.

from those that life itself depends upon to frivolous kinds of wants, the lack of which would render only a slight discomfort.[26]

> Here then we have reached the goal of the present inquiry, and may formulate it thus: the value of a good is measured by the importance of that concrete want, or partial want, which is *least urgent* among the wants that are met from the available stock of similar goods. What determines the value of a good, then is not its greatest utility, not its average utility, but the least utility which it, or one like it, might be reasonably employed in providing under the concrete economical conditions. To save ourselves the repetition of this circumstantial description . . . we shall follow Wieser in calling this least utility . . . the utility that stands on the margin of the economically permissible . . . the economic Marginal Utility of the good. The law which governs amount of value, then, may be put in the following very simple form: The value of a good is determined by the amount of its Marginal Utility.[27]

This principle, according to Böhm-Bawerk, "is not only the keystone of the theory of value, but, as affording the explanation of all economic transactions, it is the keystone of all economic theory."[28] Just how much of a keystone this theory is in neoclassical economics remains to be seen.

There is, as Professor Robbins claims, no direct use of pleasure and pain in this Austrian version of utilitarianism.[29] The Austrians did not unequivocally endorse Bentham as did W. S. Jevons.[30] Nevertheless, there is no doubt about the identity of meaning of Jevons and the Austrians. Both assume a human nature so constituted that there is in each individual a series of graded sensations or pleasures. Things are valued in accordance with the relative duration and intensity of sensation derived from the contemplation of the consumption of that good. This is hedonism. But it is the pleasure side of the hedonic calculus that is being emphasized. Man is still a creature whose actions can be understood in terms of pleasures and pains. Unlike the classical economists, the marginal utility economists stress the pleasure aspect of hedonism. Pleasure is the dominant force in terms of which human economic behavior can be under-

26 *Ibid.*, p. 140.
27 *Ibid.*, pp. 148-149.
28 *Ibid.*, p. 149.
29 Robbins, *op. cit.*, p. 84.
30 Jevons, *op. cit.*, Chaps. I, II.

stood. General demand is simply a reflection of the series of graded sensations experienced by each member of the entire population.

Alfred Marshall has often been characterized as the great synthesizer. It is held that the classicists emphasized the supply side of the pecuniary calculus while the marginal utility economists emphasized the demand side. To the great credit of Marshall he was able to bring both of these doctrines under one unified economic structure. That Marshall was aware of his synthesizing role is clear from his introductory chapter to Book III of his *Principles.*[31] Nevertheless, Marshall's was also a synthesis of the pain of the classicist with the pleasure of the Austrian and other marginal utility economists. Marshall, although not making such a claim, brought into economic theory the unadulterated pleasure-pain calculus, as Senior had done sixty years earlier.

Marshall comes close in his analysis of wants to a behavioristic psychology, but resorts, after merely a hint of something else, to a pure hedonism. Although he claims that in primitive man wants are given, he holds that as man progresses his wants increase in number and variety. But he claims that at this later stage of society wants are the product of activity.

> Speaking broadly therefore, although it is man's wants in the earliest stages of his development that give rise to his activities, yet afterwards each new step upwards is to be regarded as the development of new activities giving rise to new wants, rather than of new wants giving rise to new activities.[32]

After this hopeful beginning Marshall resorts again to the hedonistic psychology. Demand is found to rest not on activity, but on desire or want or utility. Thus, the source of demand is utility or feelings of satisfaction. These satisfactions are subject to the law of diminishing returns. "In other words, the additional benefit which a person derives from a given increase of his stock of a thing, diminishes with every increase in the stock that he already has."[33] Satisfaction is what Marshall means by utility and he shows by this a clear acceptance of hedonism.

On the other hand, Marshall also accepts the classical expla-

---

31 Marshall, *Principles,* pp. 83-85.
32 *Ibid.,* p. 89.
33 *Ibid.,* p. 93.

nation of supply in terms of pain or, as he states it, "discommodity." Work is irksome and "whatever be the form of the discommodity, its intensity nearly always increases with the severity and the duration of labour." In other words, labor is subject to increasing disutility. But not only labor is so construed. Supply is the product of capital and labor and the accumulation of capital is accomplished under the same disutility. Marshall attempts to avoid the ridiculousness of Senior's "pain of abstinence" as an explanation of the payment of interest, but he is not too successful, for he also speaks of "labour, and the sacrifice involved in putting off consumption,"[34] and again he states:

> The exertions of all the different kinds of labour that are directly or indirectly involved in making it; together with the abstinence or rather the waiting required for saving the capital used in making it: all these efforts and sacrifices together will be called the *real cost of production* of the commodity.[35]

Supply is thus explained in hedonistic terms, both labor and capital being the product of sacrifice and pain. This is essentially the position of classical political economy once the contribution of Senior had been added.

Production thus becomes a problem in the balancing of pleasures and pains. This is quite apparent in the case of a boy picking berries.

> The simplest case of balance or equilibrium between desire and effort is found when a person satisfies one of his wants by his own direct work. When a boy picks blackberries for his own eating, the action of picking is probably itself pleasurable for a while; and for some time longer, the pleasure of eating is more than enough to repay the trouble of picking. But after he has eaten a good deal, the desire for more diminishes; while the task of picking begins to cause weariness, which may indeed be a feeling of monotony rather than of fatigue. Equilibrium is reached when at last his eagerness to play and his disinclination for the work of picking counterbalances the desire for eating. The satisfaction which he can get from picking fruit has arrived at its maximum: for up to that time, every fresh picking has added more to his pleasure than it has taken away; and after that time any further picking would take away from his pleasure more than it would add.[36]

34 *Ibid.*, p. 140.
35 *Ibid.*, p. 339.
36 *Ibid.*, p. 331.

From this account of human behavior in terms of an equilibrium of pleasure and pain, Marshall advances the analysis through barter to a money economy. The major portion of his *Principles* is devoted to an exposition of the pleasure-pain calculus on the societal level in a pecuniary economy.[37] Professor Pigou in his *Economics of Welfare* has built upon the hedonistic calculus in much the same manner except that he has shown that a maximization of individual self-interest—or net pleasure—does not always result in the maximization of the best interests—or pleasures—of society.[38]

Except for further mathematical analysis, and the injection of monopolistic competition, classical economics has remained down to the present time as Marshall left it. Certainly the psychology underlying an analysis of production in cost (supply) and desire (demand) terms has not undergone any change. Those classicists who have been sensitive to the criticisms of the hedonistic psychology have frequently taken the position of Professor Robbins as indicated in an earlier quotation.[39] Such economic analysis has concentrated on a study of price relationships and points of equilibria under competition and monopoly with no reference to the underlying psychology. Nevertheless, the hedonistic psychology is implied. Simply ignoring the underlying psychological preconceptions, as Professor Robbins proposes, does not rid the theoretical structure of these preconceptions. One contemporary neoclassicist has stated this obvious truth as follows:

> Indeed it is impossible to explain even the determination of prices without some reference to the concept of well-being. In attempting to define the quantity of any commodity we are constantly forced to recognize that commodities are wanted not for their own sakes but for the sake of some satisfaction derived from their use or consumption.[40]

Present day classical economists are prone to make the assumption that economic activity is understandable in terms

37 *Ibid.*, Books III, IV, and V, pp. 83-503.

38 A. C. Pigou, *The Economics of Welfare*, London, Macmillan, 1924, part II, Chaps. I-IV.

39 See above, pp. 39-40.

40 Boulding, *Economic Analysis*, p. 9.

of maximization.[41] By this means all reference to psychology is avoided, and thus criticism is avoided on this score. Nevertheless, the assumption of maximization has meaning only in terms of hedonism. For what is being maximized? It can only be utility or want-satisfaction. This is the real meaning of the matter. Hedonism has simply been hidden. The real significance of the analysis of production in terms of marginal cost and marginal revenue is that it purports to show under what conditions a maximum of want-satisfaction is obtained and under what conditions it is not.

All this may seem to be belaboring a point that has too frequently been made. Many have criticized the classicist for clinging to hedonism. But what is significant is not only the invalidity of hedonism. The present inquiry is concerned with change in classical economic theory; and for this inquiry it is especally significant that hedonism furnishes a base for the whole Newtonian conception of mechanical change that characterizes classical political economy.

Bentham, who first formalized hedonism as a social doctrine, was a product of that same Newtonian eighteenth century that produced Adam Smith. One of the aims of Bentham was to formulate a science of human behavior that would have the scientific authenticity of the Newtonian mechanics.[42] Whether or not he succeeded in this, there is a resemblance between his conception of human behavior and Newton's conception of the universe. Motion in both cases is a product of abstract force operating on an opaque agent, always directed toward the establishment of an equilibrium of counteracting forces. Thus, hedonism is Newtonianism applied to human behavior, and the Newtonian concept of mechanical change is used hedonically to explain motion in human behavior.

It is this concept of a passive human agent that differentiates hedonism from later types of psychological theory. A conception of man as an initiator of action is the one thing that later psychologies such as instinct, behaviorist, Freudian, and

[41] For example see, Lorie Tarshis, *The Elements of Economics,* New York, Houghton Mifflin, 1947, pp. 29-30.

[42] Wesley Mitchell, *Lecture Notes on Types of Economic Theory,* New York, Augustus Kelley, 1949, Vol. I, pp. 95-96.

Gestalt hold in common, and it is the one thing that sets these more modern psychologies off from hedonism. In fact the abandonment of the words pleasure and pain by the economist was not sufficient to modernize hedonistic psychology, for the major objection to hedonism was not to be found in the use of the words pleasure and pain. The major objection to this psychology is its conception of the human being as a passive agent, a mere receptor of pleasures and pains.

Economic theory on either the individual or the societal level has been an attempt to explain how man achieves a minimum of pain and a maximum of satisfaction. This is what Professor Robbins means when he states that "Economics is the science which studies human behavior as a relationship between ends and scarce means which have alternative uses."[43] Although he claims that "Equilibrium is just equilibrium,"[44] the reason for his concern and that of other classical economists is because it is not "just equilibrium." It has significance because of its basis in hedonism.

But more is involved than equilibrium. Hedonism views life as directed toward certain consummatory ends, and economic theory has been a reflection of the hedonistic conception of the nature of man. Economic activity has been conceived as directed to an ultimate end in consumption. Theory has inquired how this end can be achieved with a minimum of pain, and result in a maximum of pleasure. As a consequence, economic activity is a discrete series of production and consummation problems. Change is conceived as a consequence of disturbing elements that prevent this end from being achieved. The conceptions both of human nature and of change are Newtonian in character. Change amounts to activity directed to re-establishment of a broken equilibrium, and equilibrium means a balance of pleasure and pain. Despite denials by those classicists such as Robbins who are embarrassed by hedonism and attempt to avoid the accusation by ignoring psychology, the psychological preconceptions are apparent and they have far-reaching consequences in economic theory. They are of great significance in the classicist's theory of change—a return to a lost equilibrium, meaning to a new hedonistic balance.

---

43 Robbins, *op. cit.*, p. 16.

44 *Ibid.*, p. 143.

Unlike the contemporary classicist who denies the relevancy of psychology, the institutionalist lays great stress on the importance of psychology to economic theory.[45] Economic theory is a science of human behavior, and it cannot slough off psychology by concentrating on price analysis *in vacuo*. Prices and the "price system" have no meaning except in terms of human behavior; they are manifestations of a culturally conditioned pattern. Since this is the case, the institutionalist argues that psychology is essential to economic theory and that the psychology must be in conformance "with the analysis of behavior generally."[46]

This idea is not a contradiction of the position of the early classical economist, for his economic theory was based on a conception of human behavior that was explicit in his theory. There are psychological preconceptions in both types of theory. There is, however, a great divergence between the conceptions of human behavior held by each. Moreover, these psychological preconceptions affect the entire character of the economic theory of each and are of great significance in explaining their different conceptions of change. Following our examination of the psychology of the classicist and its influence on his concept of economic change, it remains to examine the psychology of the institutionalist and to show how it is related to his theory of economic change.

Between the time of Bentham and the development of institutional economics in the twentieth century, much was learned about human behavior that was not available to the Benthamites. Later conceptions of human behavior were based more on empirical research and less on common-sense notions of human motivation than those of an earlier day. People like William James, trained in medical science, had turned their attention to human behavior with the result that notions of human behavior that had been accepted as common sense were subjected to scientific scrutiny. Through the work of Comte, Spencer, and later sociologists, attention was focused on the group aspect of human behavior. In addition, the notion of the savage—held by Rousseau and other seventeenth- and eighteenth-century philosophers and accepted by all engaged

45 C. E. Ayres, *The Theory of Economic Progress*, p. 89.
46 John Gambs, *Beyond Supply and Demand*, pp. 27-28.

in social inquiry—was subjected to a rude jolt by the inquiries of the anthropologist. All of these factors contributed in turn to the development of a new concept of human nature.

As was explained above, the common-sense psychology viewed the human agent as a receptor of sensations who was moved to action by these sensations. Without the sensations or feelings, no action took place. The "new psychology," or psychologies, conceived the human agent as an actor, and activity rather than sensations became the center of attention.[47] Sensation was held to be something that accompanied action and was not held to be the cause of action. Activity was primary and sensation was of importance only as it influenced further activity. Man was a creature of motor impulses that result in a continuous series of activities.

> The idea of a thing intrinsically wholly inert in the sense of absolutely passive is expelled from physics and has taken refuge in the psychology of current economics. In truth man acts anyway, he can't help acting. In every fundamental sense it is false that a man requires a motive to make him do something. To a healthy man inaction is the greatest of woes. Any one who observed children knows that while periods of rest are natural, laziness is an acquired vice—or virtue. While a man is awake he will do something, if only to build castles in the air.[48]

From this conception of human nature it follows that motive is no longer of such importance as it was for older psychologies, especially hedonism. Since man is a creature of constant action, it is activity itself that is of significance. As Dewey has said,

> There is doubtless some sense in saying that every conscious act has an incentive or motive. But this sense is as truistic as that of the not dissimilar saying that every event has a cause. Neither statement throws any light on any particular occurrence.[49]

The question on which the student of human behavior centers his attention is, what channels these motor impulses into identifiable patterns of human behavior?

This question directs attention to the social structure and its influence in molding human behavior. As Charles Cooley

47 Horace M. Kallen, "Behaviorism," *Encyclopedia of the Social Sciences*, Vol. II, pp. 495-498.

48 John Dewey, *Human Nature and Conduct*, New York, Modern Library, 1930, pp. 118-119.

49 *Ibid.*, p. 118.

so well demonstrated with his "looking-glass self," human behavior is social behavior, and the individual personality or accumulation of habit patterns is a product of a particular social environment.[50] Motor impulses give rise to activity, but the particular form of this activity is dependent upon the cultural milieu.

This thought was revolutionary so far as the concept of human nature was concerned. To the common-sense psychology, the social universe was a reflection of a constant human nature. But to the "new psychology" human nature was a product of the social order.[51] This idea is central to Dewey's *Human Nature and Conduct* and is reiterated throughout the volume. In one passage Dewey states,

> In short, the *meaning* of native activities is not native; it is acquired. It depends upon interaction with a matured social medium. In the case of a tiger or eagle, anger may be identified with a serviceable life-activity, with attack and defense. With a human being it is as meaningless as a gust of wind on a mudpuddle apart from a direction given it by the presence of other persons, apart from the response they make to it. It is a physical spasm, a blind dispersive burst of wasteful energy. It gets quality, significance, when it becomes a smouldering sullenness, an annoying interruption, a peevish irritation, a murderous revenge, a blazing indignation. And although these phenomena which have a meaning spring from original native reactions to stimuli, yet they depend also upon the responsive behavior of others. They and all similar human displays of anger are not pure impulses, they are *habits* formed under the influence of association with others who have habits already and who show their habits in the treatment which converts a blind physical discharge into a significant anger.[52]

This way of viewing human behavior has been clearly stated by an anthropologist in a recent volume. Leslie White does not deny the importance of the neuro-sensory structures of the human species, but he does state clearly that actual patterns of human behavior cannot be explained by this structure. Behavior is understandable only in terms of the cultural milieu in which that behavior takes place.

---

[50] C. H. Cooley, *Human Nature and the Social Order*, New York, Charles Scribner's Sons, 1902, Chap. V.

[51] J. F. Brown, *Psychology and the Social Order*, New York, McGraw-Hill, 1936, Chap. XIV, "The Original Nature of Man."

[52] Dewey, *op. cit.*, p. 90.

We see then that any given specimen of human behavior is made up of two distinct factors proceeding from separate and independent sources. On the one hand is the organism, composed of bones, muscles, nerves, glands, and sense organs. This organism is a single coherent unit, a system, with definite properties of its own. On the other hand is the cultural tradition into which the organism is born. There is, of course, no necessary relation between the infant organism and the particular type of culture into which it is born. It could have been born into one cultural tradition as well as another, into Tibetan as well as American or Eskimoan culture. But, from the standpoint of subsequent behavior, everything depends upon the type of culture into which the baby is introduced by birth. If he is born into one culture he will think, feel and act in one way; if into another, his behavior will be correspondingly different. Human behavior is, therefore, always and everywhere, made up of these two ingredients; the dynamic organization of nerves, glands, muscles, and sense organs, that is *man,* and the extrasomatic cultural tradition.[53]

The new psychology holds that human behavior is subject to a process of cumulative growth and adaptation. It is through activity that habits are formed and behavior takes on character. But these habits are the product of past activity and, since they are established through activity, they are subject to modification and change with continued activity.[54] In fact Dewey places great emphasis on the role of intelligence in activity as it modifies habitual behavior.[55] Thus, human behavior is subject to a process of cumulative change and development and adaptation. This whole way of viewing human behavior is a product of the Darwinian revolution in human thought. It represents Darwinism translated into the analysis of human behavior.

Institutionalism has absorbed this behavioristic psychology. In fact, institutionalist economics and behaviorist psychology have developed out of the same environment and have had a parallel development. It is not strange then that the institutionalist psychology is that of behaviorism. In fact, as will be shown, the behaviorist psychology of the institutionalist gives to institutionalist economics the peculiar Darwinian flavor which is its dominant characteristic.

[53] Leslie White, *The Science of Culture,* New York, Farrar Straus, and Co., 1949, Chap. 6, "Culturological vs. Psychological Interpretations of Human Behavior," pp. 122-123.

[54] Robert S. Woodworth, *Psychology,* New York, Holt, 1934, pp. 158-178.

[55] Dewey, *op. cit.,* pp. 172-180.

Despite the fact that institutionalism claims behaviorism,[56] critics have claimed that institutionalist economics falls down because of its acceptance of the refuted instinct psychology. This criticism is leveled largely because of the use of instinct by Veblen, particularly in his *Instinct of Workmanship*. But the criticisms have never gone much beyond a superficial examination of his use of instinct. A more careful examination of the Veblenian use of this term makes clear that Veblen has closer ties to behaviorist than to instinct psychology.[57]

There is a decided difference between Veblen's use of the term "instinct" and that of an instinct psychologist such as William James. To James, "Instinct is usually defined as the faculty of acting in such a way as to produce certain ends, without foresight of the ends, and without previous education in the performance."[58] James accounts for changes in patterns of behavior over the life span of the individual by what he calls the "law of transitoriness," by which he holds that "Many instincts ripen at a certain age and then fade away."[59] In addition instinctive behavior is modifiable by thought of consequences to follow, once the consequences of instinctive behavior have been felt. "An insect that lays her eggs in a place when she never sees them hatched must always do so 'blindly'; but a hen who has already hatched a brood can hardly be assumed to sit with perfect 'blindness' on her second nest."[60] Nevertheless, except for these modifications, to James behavior was a thing fixed by the complex instinctive makeup of mankind.

But to Veblen, instinct has a different meaning. Attention has been called by Joseph Dorfman to the fact that Veblen was quite well aware of this difference and that he used instinct in a rather vague manner.[61] It is unfortunate that Veblen nowhere defined instinct. The closest he comes to a definition is in a passage in the *Instinct of Workmanship* in which he states that,

---

56 Ayres, *op. cit.*, p. 89.

57 S. M. Daugert, *The Philosophy of Thorstein Veblen*, New York, Columbia University Press, 1950, pp. 74-77.

58 William James, *Psychology*, Cleveland, World Publishing Co., 1948, p. 391.

59 *Ibid.*, p. 402.

60 *Ibid.*, p. 395.

61 Joseph Dorfman, *Thorstein Veblen and His America*, p. 324.

All instinctive behavior is subject to development and hence to modification by habit. Such impulsive action as is in no degree intelligent and so suffers no adaptation through habitual use, is not properly to be called instinctive; it is rather to be classed as tropismatic."[62]

In this statement Veblen classes that type of behavior as "tropismatic" which James called "instinctive." Although he here defines tropismatic behavior rather clearly, he has still left undefined what he means by instinctive behavior. Nevertheless, Veblen, by leaving the way open for modifications of instinctive behavior by habit, comes close to the concept of human behavior held by Dewey. Impulse or instinct is not the major center of attention. The major interest is in activity and how the total environment modifies and shapes human behavior. In other words, instinct is treated much as the behaviorist treats impulse. The neuro-sensory-muscular make-up of man is essential to human activity in general, but specific human behavior is a product of the cultural milieu. Veblen's handling of instinct is just in these terms. It is not instinct that determines the social and cultural environment, but the social and cultural environment determine the type and mode of behavior in which instinct manifests itself. This is what Veblen meant by his statement that "instinctive behavior is subject to development and hence to modification by habit."

This becomes clearer in Veblen's economic theory. In his analysis of economic behavior, Veblen holds that man is possessed of propensities such as the instinct of workmanship, the parental bent, and exploit. In fact the first two have been frequently subordinated to the last in the development of human culture. Nevertheless, there is never any doubt that Veblen's main attention is upon the cultural development of mankind and how behavior, in origin instinctive or impulsive, has been shaped by the cultural situation.

In the relatively peaceful savage society, the instinct of workmanship and the parental bent are allowed free reign. The result is the development of matter-of-fact knowledge, evidenced by the domestication of plants and animals. All of this development works out to the advancement of the well-

62 Thorstein Veblen, *The Instinct of Workmanship and the State of the Industrial Arts,* New York, B. W. Huebsch, 1922, p. 38.

being of the human species. In this culture man is essentially of the same biological make-up as man at a later cultural development. But because of the peaceable nature of society and the relative lack of coercion, the instinct of workmanship is allowed to work itself out in patterns of behavior that conduce to material advancement. The propensity to exploit is in the biological make-up of the savage man, but his culture is such that it is relatively dormant. Exploit does not manifest itself in an elaborate set of behavior patterns. The dominant modes of thought run in terms of fertility and workmanship.[63]

The workmanship of the savage society makes possible the domestication of plants and animals, which results in the production of an economic surplus. Under this condition the predatory aspect of human behavior asserts itself, as there is here a surplus to be engrossed by chicane and exploit. In these circumstances that aspect of human nature called exploit asserts itself and human behavior becomes dominated by exploit. Workmanship is bent to making exploit more successful.[64] Conspicuous waste and conspicuous consumption are developed as a means of demonstrating successful predation.[65] Ownership and the leisure class arise simultaneously with the passage from the savage to the barbaric culture.[66] In other words, a change in the cultural circumstances alters the instincts that are uppermost in originating human behavior.

Veblen holds that the cultural conditions must be such as to provide a sufficiently peaceable atmosphere for workmanship to assert itself. Thus, modern industrialism was carried by workmanship to a high order of development in the British Isles. The insular position of the British Isles protected the British against the predatory activity of the dynastic states on the continent of Europe. Secured from predation and military free-booting, the British developed the industrialism they had borrowed from the low countries. These same low countries did not develop this industrialism to the extent that the British did because they were subjected to the constant predation of

63 *Ibid.*, pp. 103-137.

64 *Ibid.*, pp. 146-170.

65 Thorstein Veblen, *The Theory of the Leisure Class*, New York, Modern Library, 1934, pp. 35-101.

66 Veblen, *The Instinct of Workmanship*, pp. 146-147; *The Theory of the Leisure Class*, p. 22.

the dynastic states and because of the bellicose frame of mind that indulgence in such activity generated.[67] In other words, the extremely predatory culture of the mainland of Europe worked against the full operation of workmanship and the rise in material well-being in which its free working results. On the other hand, the British, free from such activity, provided a cultural setting in which workmanship could develop relatively untrammeled.

Veblen held that the racial make-up of modern man was essentially that of early neolithic man. No mutational change in the racial composition of mankind had taken place since that time. Nevertheless, human behavior had been noticeably different throughout the passage of time from the neolithic peoples to modern times. Since there had been no significant change in race, the difference had to be explained in terms of culture. Although man might be a creature of "instincts" or "impulses," the mode of behavior in which these "instincts" were manifested varied greatly. Thus the implication is that behavior patterns must be explained in terms of cultural evolution and not instinct. Nevertheless, the nature of man is important if for nothing else than that it sets an outer-limit to human behavior.

That Veblen did not hold that culture forms could be explained by the instinctive nature of man is clear from his treatment of England and Germany in *Imperial Germany and the Industrial Revolution*. In this volume he states explicitly in the very beginning that these two peoples are of similar racial stock.

> In point of race the population of south Germany is substantially identical with that of northern France or the neighboring parts of Belgium; while in the same respect the population of north Germany has substantially the same composition as that of Holland and Denmark on the west and of western Russia on the east; and taking the Fatherland as a whole, its population is in point of race substantially identical with that of the British Isles.[68]

Since this is the case, the cultural differences between these peoples must be accounted for in terms of the evolution of

---

67 Veblen, *The Instinct of Workmanship*, pp. 249-253.

68 Thorstein Veblen, *Imperial Germany and the Industrial Revolution*, New York, Viking, 1946, p. 8.

culture itself. This is precisely what Veblen does in *Imperial Germany*. Not only that, but he shows that the industrial organization modified human behavior and the habitual outlook of the British. A less bellicose frame of mind came to prevail in England.[69] Germany borrowed the material culture of the British, but since those attitudes and habits of thought that had been developed with the new industrial technology were not borrowed, the industrial technology had a different effect in Germany. The Germans, being of a more archaic frame of mind in which exploit in its crudest form was dominant, put the machine technology to the service of the aggrandizement of the dynastic state. Exploit in the use of technology in the German culture was not the product of the peculiar German racial make-up. It was a product of the cultural background of the German peoples.

If the use of the word instinct by Veblen has led some people to classify him as a follower of the instinct school, there is certainly no reason for neglecting that aspect of his thought on human behavior in which his identification with behaviorism is clear-cut. Nowhere does he more clearly identify himself with the behaviorists than in the following passage.

The later psychology, reinforced by modern anthropological research, gives a different conception of human nature. According to this conception, it is the characteristic of man to do something, not simply to suffer pleasures and pains through the impact of suitable forces. He is not simply a bundle of desires that are to be saturated by being placed in the path of the forces of the environment, but rather a coherent structure of propensities and habits which seeks realization and expression in an unfolding activity. According to this view, human activity, and economic activity among the rest, is not apprehended as something incidental to the process of saturating given desires. The activity is itself the substantial fact of the process, and the desires under whose guidance the action takes place are circumstances of temperament which determine the specific direction in which the activity will unfold itself in the given case. These circumstances of temperament are ultimate and definitive for the individual who acts under them, so far as regards his attitude as agent in the particular action in which he is engaged. But, in the view of the science, they are elements of the existing frame of mind of the agent, and are the outcome of his antecedents and his life up to the point at which he stands. They are the products of his heredi-

69 *Ibid.*, pp. 88-120.

tary traits and his past experience, cumulatively wrought out under a given body of traditions, conventionalities, and material circumstances; and they afford the point of departure for the next step in the process. The economic life history of the individual is a cumulative process of adaptation of means to ends that cumulatively change as the process goes on, both the agent and his environment being at any point the outcome of the last process. His methods of life to-day are enforced upon him by his habits of life carried over from yesterday and by the circumstances left as the mechanical residue of the life of yesterday.[70]

There is a remarkable similarity between this passage and the concept of human behavior held by Dewey and others of the more modern behaviorist school.[71] This passage shows that when Veblen was not injecting the word "instinct" into the discussion, he was a behaviorist. But like that of all behaviorists, his concept of human action was Darwinian. The behavior of the individual is held to be subject to a process of cumulative change and development.

Veblen's psychological preconceptions are those of all institutionalists. Institutionalist economics is not based on an instinct psychology. It is behaviorist and, thus, Darwinian. No institutionalist since Veblen, with the exception of Carleton Parker,[72] has resorted to the use of instinct. Yet valuable work has been done using essentially the same concept of human behavior as used by Veblen.

Unlike the classicist who assumed a relatively fixed and relatively simple human nature, the institutionalist views human behavior as a complex of neuro-sensory activity guided in its outward manifestation by the total cultural situation. Hoxie in his work on trade unionism emphasized this aspect of human behavior. He claimed that "man is a product of his total social environment and inheritance."[73] Allan Gruchy reiterates approximately the same idea in his recent volume on institutional

70 Thorstein Veblen, *The Place of Science in Modern Civilization*, pp. 74-75.

71 For a similar short passage see John Dewey, *Reconstruction in Philosophy*, Boston, Beacon, 1948, pp. 84-90.

72 Carleton H. Parker, *The Casual Laborer and Other Essays*, New York, Harcourt, Brace and Co., 1920. Parker adopted the instinct psychology in an unadulterated form. He attempted to list the instincts and got into the same difficulty as the instinct psychologists.

73 R. F. Hoxie, *Trade Unionism in the United States*, New York, D. Appleton and Co., 1917, p. 368. For his detailed discussion of human behavior see Chap. XIV, "Social Control."

economics. Gruchy, like Commons, stresses the collective nature of human behavior and the changing character of collective behavior.[74]

In the work of Commons a similar psychology is apparent. Although he calls it a volitional psychology, it is certainly akin to behaviorism. In Commons' system the individual is an active agent guided by some end-in-view.[75] Although he uses the term will, which is looked upon with some scepticism by modern psychologists, it is clear that he uses it to convey the same meaning that Veblen did when he claimed that all human behavior is directed toward some desired goal. Commons also holds that this individual action is shaped by the group to which the individual belongs. The molds which give individual action a collective aspect are the working rules. Even though he does not make use of the term culture, it is apparent from Commons' use of working rules that it is very close to what the anthropologist calls mores and folkways.[76] Commons nowhere makes as wide use of the institutions-technology dichotomy as Veblen did, but it is apparent, as will be brought out later, that Commons had glimmerings of this characteristic of human behavior.

The most recent full analysis of the nature of human behavior by an institutional economist has been that of C. E. Ayres in his *Theory of Economic Progress.* Ayres uses the earlier dichotomy of Veblen in which social behavior is held to have two aspects that are continuous and related but distinct. These two aspects of behavior were noted by Veblen in some of his earlier essays. Veblen claimed that man manifested an ability to view phenomena in matter-of-fact terms as well as animistically. In the first case the result was technology which Veblen defined as "the employment of scientific knowledge for useful ends." He defined technology broadly as including "besides the machine industry proper, such branches of practice as engineering, agriculture, medicine, sanitation, and economic reform."[77] In these activities workmanship prevails and

[74] Allan Gruchy, *Modern Economic Thought,* pp. 560-565.

[75] Commons, *op. cit.,* pp. 36-42. See also "Introduction" by Kenneth H. Parsons, pp. 9-18.

[76] *Ibid.,* pp. 26-27.

[77] Thorstein Veblen, *The Place of Science in Modern Civilization,* p. 16.

technological patterns of behavior arise. But, in addition, man has a tendency to view things animistically, imputing mystic potencies to phenomena and to individuals held to be capable of working feats of mystery. Invidious distinctions have been drawn between individuals of different status or roles according to the quantity of mystic potency held by one of such a status. Ceremonial behavior patterns develop around imposition and investiture of status. These two aspects of behavior patterns are related, but all behavior has distinct ceremonial and technological aspects.

Ayres has developed this dichotomy, joining together the work of Veblen and that of John Dewey. Human behavior is social behavior and can only be understood in terms of culture.[78] It exhibits technological and ceremonial aspects. Technological patterns of behavior are subject to a cumulative process of growth and development.[79] Ceremonial patterns are relatively fixed and subject to change only through a break in the continuity of the culture in which they exist. They are not subject to a process of cumulative development.[80] In this analysis, which is similar to that of Veblen, the matter of instinct is left out with no deleterious effects on the analysis. The neurosensory mechanism is taken for granted and the center of attention is culture and cultural behavior. It is held by Ayres, as by most institutionalists, that the biological make-up of man does not explain patterns of behavior. In order to understand human behavior, attention must center on culture.[81]

Thus, to the institutionalist, behavior cannot be explained on an "individual" basis. There is no such thing as individual behavior. All behavior is cultural. Culture is subject to a process of cumulative development and change, and human behavior is therefore subject to this same process. Economic behavior, like all behavior, is subject to continued cumulative change and since the center of attention of the institutionalist is human behavior, his whole economic structure assumes a Darwinian complexion. To the institutionalist the individual is active, but he acts within a specific developing cultural pattern. Allan

---

78 Ayres, *The Theory of Economic Progress*, pp. 89-96.
79 *Ibid.*, Chap. VI.
80 *Ibid.*, Chap. VIII.
81 *Ibid.*, p. 96.

Gruchy has called attention to this aspect of institutionalist theory.

> What this new psychological interpretation involves is a fresh interpretation of that original human nature which is itself so impervious to change.
>
> The assumptions of the holistic economists relating to the nature of human behavior are in conformity with their view of the economic system as an evolving cultural complex. Their psychology of adjustment and adaptation is useful in explaining human behavior in an economic world in which technological innovation has a very important role to play.[82]

The effect of this concept of human behavior on economic theory and its importance to the institutionalist have been noted by John Gambs as well as Gruchy.[83]

Since the institutionalist has centered his attention on human behavior that is culturally determined, he has developed a Darwinian science in which change is of central importance. This could not have been done until the tools for recognizing cultural change were available. In fact it was not until the second half of the last century that the concept "culture" was available for use in social analysis.[84] But once the concepts of culture and of the culture trait and culture complex, as well as of folkways and mores, were developed, the tools were available for recognizing the process of cumulative change in human behavior as well as the static side of that behavior. Culture is subject to cumulative change. Thus, human behavior changes and what has traditionally been subsumed under "human nature" is likewise subject to change. Institutionalism developed at a time when these tools of analysis were still being refined and the institutionalist used them effectively to analyze economic behavior. The results are to be seen in his analysis of the social structure as well as in his concept of progress.

In summary, it can be said that classical economic psychology holds the individual to be acted upon in much the same manner as the celestial bodies are acted upon by the forces of gravity. The hedonistic psychology of the classicists assumed

---

82 Gruchy, *op. cit.*, p. 565.
83 Gambs, *op. cit.*, p. 30.
84 White, *The Science of Culture*, p. 87.

a fixed human nature. Activity was the result of a disequilibrium of pleasures and pains and was a striving toward a re-establishment of a lost equilibrium. This activity resulted in no fundamental change, individual or social. Change was only from a pleasurable balance to an unpleasant balance and back to a pleasurable balance again.

Institutionalism, on the other hand, views the individual as an active agent, acting upon his environment, making adjustments. To the institutionalist, the actor is subject to permanent alteration by a cumulative series of actions. In fact the actor becomes the product of the cumulative series.

The difference between the two schools in their concepts of change is manifested in their psychology. The classical concept of human nature is in conformance with Newtonian concepts of mechanistic change while that of the institutionalist is in conformance with the Darwinian concept of cumulative and nonteleological change. But these differences in concepts of change are also apparent in other phases of their economic theory. We will now turn to an analysis of the concepts of society to which these concepts of human nature are related.

IV

CHANGE AND SOCIAL ORGANIZATION

The concepts of society and social organization manifest in classical and institutional theory throw further light on their concepts of change. To the classicist, social organization is fixed, and the status groups represented by capitalist, landlord, and laborer reflect a natural order. To the institutionalist, the social organization, at present characterized by capitalist, landlord, and laborer, is and has been subject to continual change, and at any point of time it reflects a particular set of conditions.

The fixed nature of the social universe in classical theory follows from the conception of human nature held by the classicist. The individual is held to be a rational calculator of sensations of pleasure and pain. Capitalist social organization seems to be a reflection of rational human nature. As one writer has stated,

> The moral philosophers of the eighteenth century believed the institutions of their day to be an expression of divine wisdom as made manifest in human nature, and the orthodox economists of the twentieth century still adhere to this belief; that is, they willingly confine their discussion to the framework afforded by prevailing institutions because they conceive the institutions to be an expression of human nature. The institutionalists decline to do so because they hold precisely the opposite view of human nature, to wit, that it is the expression of institutions.[1]

To the classicist, society is nothing more than the sum of the individuals and their actions. Since these actions are a product of hedonistic calculation, society is virtually a sum of hedonistic actions. The status groups making up that society are the product of rational calculation. Since human nature is assumed to be primary and constant, this conception of society does not postulate continuous change.

As has been frequently pointed out, Smith's work is a reflection of the emerging commercial society of his time. But in addition to all of this, the eighteenth century was the century of enlightenment. The philosopher of the eighteenth century

[1] C. E. Ayres, "Fifty Years Development in Ideas of Human Nature and Motivation," *American Economic Review,* XXVI, No. 1, Supplement, pp. 234-235.

prided himself on his freedom from the religio-mystic social beliefs of the medieval Scholastic. Greatly influenced by Newtonian physics, as was noted earlier, he attempted to find the natural explanation and natural laws of social organization. The eighteenth-century philosopher believed that the absence of political restraint would result in the formation of an economic organization in conformance with the original nature of man. A society formed in the absence of conscious political restraint was "natural." Smith in his monumental treatise attempted to find those natural social laws which determined the wealth of nations. Throughout the work the dominant assumption, both explicit and implicit, is that if everyone is left to seek his own self-interest in accordance with human nature, the increased material welfare of the nation will be assured. The human nature of man will work itself out through natural law to an end which is "no part of its intention."

Pecuniary pursuits flourish in the absence of restraint. The pecuniary interests, merchants, bankers, tradesmen, and manufacturers, who had been of secondary importance in feudal society, became the dominant class in the new order. Their chief concern was to operate without the restraints that had characterized feudal society and that had been characteristic of the mercantilism of the early dynastic state. In assuming that the absence of restraint was "natural," economists, such as Smith, reflected the dominant opinion of the times. The attitude of the merchant converged with that of the natural philosopher. The society dominated by the merchant class was assumed to be a "natural" one. The remaining task of the economist was to determine the laws that governed this natural society.[2] This is what Adam Smith set out to do.

Nowhere in classical theory is this point clearer than in the work of Ricardo. Without any hesitation Ricardo accepted the existent social order as it stood. The sole purpose of his inquiry is to elucidate the laws that determine the proportion of the annual income received by each of three classes, "the proprietor of the land, the owner of the stock or capital necessary for its

---

2 Arnold Toynbee, *Lectures on the Industrial Revolution of the Eighteenth Century in England*, London, Longmans, Green, 1908, pp. 64-65.

cultivation, and the labourers by whose industry it is cultivated."[3] To Ricardo these classes were peculiar to any mature civilization and their existence was taken for granted. These categories do not change. What does change or differ is the soil fertility, capital accumulation, population growth and size, and the techniques and tools employed in agriculture.[4] All of these factors that influence the wealth of a nation are important only because they are the determinants of the precise return going to each of the fixed classes. Changes in these factors make no change in the social structure.

Although the implicit assumption of the Ricardian system is the advent of the stationary state, Ricardo does not question the continuation of landlord, capitalist, and laborer at any point in his treatise. Accepting the Malthusian population doctrine, and the labor-quantity theory of value, Ricardo completed a unique but simple system. Commodities are exchanged in accordance with the quantity of labor necessary to their production.[5] Land is limited in amount and in fertility. This means that there is a diminished return per additional unit of labor on a given piece of land and that the return per unit of labor on new marginal lands is a diminishing quantity.[6] This means that as population increases, subsistence increases in value; for it absorbs more and more labor in its production. This forces up money and proportional wages; for the laborers' wage tends toward the natural price of labor, "that price which is necessary to enable the labourers . . . to subsist and to perpetuate their race, without either increase or diminution."[7] But as proportional wages rise, profits fall.[8] Profits are paid from the surplus produced by labor, and thus an increase in the proportion of marginal product accruing to wages will reduce profits. In the course of time, then, money wages and rents will rise, and profits will fall, while real wages will fall, profits will fall, and corn rents will rise.

Although Ricardo sets up a society of classes with conflicting

3 David Ricardo, *The Principles of Political Economy and Taxation*, p. 1.
4 *Loc. cit.*
5 *Ibid.*, pp. 6-7.
6 *Ibid.*, p. 37.
7 *Ibid.*, p. 52.
8 *Ibid.*, pp. 64-65.

interests, he did not see any prospect of change in the class structure of that society. Ricardian socialists such as Thompson and Hodgskin as well as Marx did see the class conflicts in the Ricardian system, and used them to demonstrate the change that would take place in the class structure of economic society. But Ricardo, true to classicism, saw the social system of his time as permanent. Wesley Mitchell has called attention to this facet of Ricardianism.

> Ricardo thought of social organization as something that had changed materially in the past, but had reached maturity and would not change materially in the future. With Adam Smith, he looked back to "that early and rude state of society which precedes both the accumulation of stock and the appropriation of land." . . . It was by the light of a capitalist reason that Ricardo saw how savages behave; a more deceptive light he could not have had.[9]

Although these assumptions of the permanency of society at the time of Ricardo are important for Ricardian theory, a much greater importance is to be found in their influence on the further course of economic theory. Ricardo, taking for granted the social relations of his time and considering only their price manifestations, concentrated his attention on distribution of income and on price or value. As a result, Ricardian economics centered the economist's attention on price, both commodity and factor price. Economic science became the study of price movements within a fixed social structure which was taken for granted.

Ever since Smith and Ricardo, the classicist has assumed a permanent social organization of landlord, capitalist, and laborer. Price movement is assumed to be a manifestation of different sensory conditions in the psychic make-up of each of these classes. The continuity of later with earlier classical theory, in this regard, is made clear in Böhm-Bawerk's elaborate attempt to demonstrate that interest is a phenomenon found in all societies at all times and places because of the peculiar psychic make-up of mankind. Böhm-Bawerk identifies capitalism with what he calls roundabout methods of production. Man is faced with the choice of satisfying wants either directly, or indirectly

[9] Wesley C. Mitchell, "Postulates and Preconceptions of Ricardian Economics," reprinted in *The Backward Art of Spending Money*, New York, McGraw-Hill, 1937, p. 207.

by using a roundabout method. The latter method is more productive[10] and is identified with capitalism.[11]

Under his definition of capitalism all men at all levels of human development have been engaged in capitalist pursuits. All men have been and are tool-using animals. As a consequence they are caught up in the roundabout method of production, and they are therefore in a capitalist system whether they know it or not.

But Böhm-Bawerk goes on to show that interest would be paid in any society. The productive process is viewed as discontinuous and is looked upon as the product of sober thought as to the advantages of roundabout production over direct production. Production is time-consuming, and the more roundabout the mode of production the longer is the time before a final product is produced. Nevertheless, the roundabout process has its advantages; for it means a greater return at some future date than could be acquired more quickly by use of more direct methods of production.

Since the productive process is time-consuming it is necessary to Böhm-Bawerk for man to store provisions in order to tide him over the time before a return is realized from a more roundabout process. Robinson Crusoe must save consumption goods in order to save "productive powers" to be devoted to the production of capital goods.

> A saving of *productive powers,* be it noted; for productive powers, and not the goods which constitute capital, are the immediate object of saving. This is an important point, which must be strongly emphasized because, in the current view, too little consideration is given to it. Man saves consumption goods, his means of enjoyment; he thus saves productive powers, and with these finally he can *produce capital.*[12]

That this conception of the origin of capital is not obsolete in economic theory is demonstrated by its recurrence in current economic texts.[13]

To Böhm-Bawerk there is no difference between a non-

---

10 Eugen von Böhm-Bawerk, *The Positive Theory of Capital,* Chap. II.

11 *Ibid.,* p. 22.

12 *Ibid.,* p. 103.

13 Taylor and Barger, *The American Economy in Operation,* Chap. 6; Paul A. Samuelson, *Economics,* pp. 42-51; Bowman and Bach, *Economic Analysis and Public Policy,* New York, Prentice-Hall, 1949, pp. 189-191.

pecuniary economy and a pecuniary economy for the creation of capital. Money complicates the process, but does not alter it. In a pecuniary economy money is saved, consumption is diminished, and more "productive power" remains for the production of capital goods. Interest is paid for saving because of the difference in value between present and future goods. This difference is because of "the different circumstances of want and provision in present and future,"[14] because of the fact that "We systematically underestimate future wants, and the goods which are to satisfy them,"[15] and because of the greater technical efficiency of present goods over future goods.[16] Interest is accounted for by the greater subjective value placed upon present goods over future goods. An agio is necessary to overcome the greater value of present over future goods.[17] Since interest is largely a psychological as well as technological phenomenon, it cannot be avoided and would be found in a socialist as well as a capitalist society.[18] Thus a phenomenon peculiar to a monetary economy is identified as natural, a product of a stable human nature and the system of production. The tool-using process itself is identified with capitalism, so that all men at all times and places are held to have been engaged in capitalist ventures.

This aspect of classical economic theory persists in the work of J. B. Clark. He, like Böhm-Bawerk, views the productive process as the manipulation and combination of land, labor, and capital. Although the classes of landlord, capitalist, and laborer are not always clearly recognized, their functions are always performed, even by isolated man. The only difference between primitive society, isolated man, and the capitalist society is in the degree of specialization. All are bound in their behavior by the same natural laws of human nature.

Clark believes in a well-balanced universe that is governed by laws which work somewhat like the physical laws of the universe. Economic phenomena, in Clark's economics, have a tendency to "gravitate." This well-ordered scheme is in a constant state of flux, tending always to a well-balanced arrangement of things. The endeavor is constantly threatened by circumstances

---

14 Böhm-Bawerk, *op. cit.*, p. 249.
15 *Ibid.*, p. 253.
16 *Ibid.*, Book V, Chap. IV.
17 *Ibid.*, p. 286.
18 *Ibid.*, Book VI, Chap. X.

that work at cross purposes to the attainment of "equilibrium under the guidance of natural law." In fact, Clark's whole scheme of economic inquiry is predicated on an acceptance of this natural-order view of the universe.[19]

The first area of economic inquiry according to Clark is that of the immutable laws governing economic activity. It is essential before proceeding to the study of the more complex economies of civilized man that an inquiry be made into the eternal laws and principles governing the economic affairs of all men. Sociology is of no value to this first inquiry, for these principles come not from sociology, but from the physical universe, from physics, biology, psychology, and chemistry.[20] Following on this inquiry economic science divides itself into two more areas. It is first essential to determine within the natural social order what Clark terms economic statics, which is largely concerned with the distribution of wealth and the natural laws governing this social phenomenon. But an inquiry into economic statics is not sufficient. There are disturbing elements that constantly work at cross purposes to the orderly functioning of these natural laws. These elements must be ferreted out and a study must be made of their delaying effect on the gravitation of the economy under the guidance of natural laws toward a static arrangement. This area of inquiry Clark calls economic dynamics.[21]

Clark's economics consists, then, of three major sub-divisions: first, the natural universe uncontaminated and unaffected by social organization; second, economic statics in which the natural laws governing economic behavior have an opportunity to work themselves out; and, third, economic dynamics in which foreign elements operate so as to prevent the logical completion of economic statics.

According to Clark the natural and timeless laws that underlie the more complex economic phenomena are based on human nature and would be as true of isolated or primitive man as of man living in a more ordered state.[22] Although isolated or primitive man may not be aware of the fact, in his efforts to secure a precarious living he is engaged in a solitary venture interpret-

---

19 J. B. Clark, *Essentials of Economic Theory,* p. 1.
20 *Ibid.,* p. 58.
21 *Loc. cit.*
22 *Ibid.,* p. 2.

able in the traditional economic terms. In his fishing operations he is engaged in labor, in the manufacture and employment of capital, and in the utilization of land. Not having had the benefits of classical political economy with which to interpret his wealth-seeking activity, he is unaware of the fact that his disposal of the results of his efforts is actually the consumption of wages, interest, and rent. Despite his general state of ignorance on these fine points, this is the actual state of things in the case of both isolated and primitive man as well as that of the more advanced state typified by capitalist organization.[23] Economic laws govern just as strictly the affairs of men whether in isolation in a primitive social organization, or in a "civilized" state of being. "The wealth of a Crusoe, that of a solitary Esquimau, and that of a pygmy in equatorial Africa have laws as well as that of a European or American employer or bondholder."[24]

What are these general all-encompassing laws which man may not evade in any state of civilization? In general terms these principles are not distinguishable from the earlier felicific calculus of the Benthamites. Clark states the situation as follows:

> In all stages of social development the economic motives that actuate men remain essentially the same. All men seek to get as much net service from material wealth as they can. The more wealth they have, other things remaining the same, the better off they are, and the more personal sacrifice they are compelled to undergo in the securing of the wealth, the worse off they are. Some of the benefit received is neutralized by the sacrifice incurred; but there is a net surplus of gains not thus cancelled by sacrifices, and the generic motive which may properly be called economic is the desire to make this surplus large.[25]

In short, social behavior and social organization to Clark are the product of timeless laws seated in human nature. There is no reference to cultural behavior. Social organization is the product of the neuro-sensory make-up of man. This being the case there is no reason to expect dissolution or change in social organization. Land, labor, and capital; landlord, laborer, and capitalist, are categories found in the nature of things, and are not merely the product of cultural evolution. In the theory of

---

23 *Loc. cit.*
24 *Ibid.*, pp. 4-5.
25 *Ibid.*, p. 39.

a classicist such as Clark social organization is held to be timeless. The task of economic theory remains the explanation of price and income movements within this fixed universe. Professor Robbins takes issue with those who claim that classical economic theory is merely the reflection of a particular social organization existing in a particular time and place. This contention of the relativity of traditional theory "can be given plausibility only by a distortion of the use of words so complete as to be utterly misleading."[26] Economic science as conceived by Robbins has a universal validity.

> No one will really question the universal applicability of such assumptions as the existence of scales of relative valuation, or of different factors of production, or of different degrees of uncertainty regarding the future, even though there may be room for dispute as to the best mode of describing their exact logical status. And no one who has really examined the kind of deductions which can be drawn from such assumptions can doubt the utility of starting from this plane. It is only failure to realize this, and a too exclusive preoccupation with the subsidiary assumptions, which can lend any countenance to the view that the laws of Economics are limited to certain conditions of time and space, that they are purely historical in character, and so on.[27]

Although this argument seems to have a common-sense plausibility when the "common sense" psychology is taken for granted, Professor Robbins like all classicists makes at least an implicit assumption as to the "natural" origin of the current economic structure.

Certainly it is not true that no one will question hedonism. Robbins rests much of his argument on the universality of a scale of relative valuations being the wellspring of human behavior. This also is untrue. What remains to be answered is why a classicist such as Professor Robbins has clung so desperately to a discredited psychology? Why has he continued to hold to a hedonistic psychology which was long ago abandoned by the psychologists? The answer is to be found in the implicit assumption that the present institutional furniture is a product of a natural human selection on a universal scale of relative valuations. This assumption is necessary to the classical explanation

---

26 Robbins, *The Nature and Significance of Economic Science*, p. 80.
27 *Ibid.*, p. 81.

of price in a monetary economy. But actually, this whole price analysis is used to explain the significance of what is already taken for granted—a market economy in which landlord, capitalist, and laborer play their subjective valuations to the hilt.

If the assumption of hedonism is not sufficient indication that Robbins accepts existing status arrangements as natural, certainly the remainder of his statement should clarify this point. According to Robbins no one would question "the existence . . . of different factors of production, or of different degrees of uncertainty regarding the future." Factors of production were injected into economic theory to explain income received by status groups peculiar to a capitalist society. Landlords, laborers, and capitalists received incomes that had to be justified. Thus, through the course of the development of economic theory, these groups were each held to be productive in themselves or to be the owners of resources that were held to be productive. A large proportion of the marginal analysis that rests on Robbins' hedonistic psychology has been devoted to a justification of income received by these various status groups. Since they received income, they must be productive. Economic theory attempted to supply a mathematically precise answer to the question, why each received what it did, by resort to the incremental analysis of calculus. But in any other economy, in which none of these institutional relationships prevailed, the whole question would be irrelevant.

Much the same line of argument can be followed to show that "uncertainty" about the future applies only to a monetary economy characterized by investment for profit. Certainty or absolute predictability is impossible. Life is an uncertain thing. Success in crossing a traffic-filled street is an uncertain thing. Success in baking a cake at a high altitude is full of uncertainty. Weather prediction is not certain. The list could be indefinitely extended. The point, however, is to make it clear that what the economist has in mind when he talks about uncertainty is a peculiar type of uncertainty. He is talking about the uncertainty of an anticipated pecuniary return from a pecuniary investment. That is the only meaning of "uncertainty" in classical economic theory, for it is injected into theory to explain investment for profit and the rate of profit. But this obviously assumes a fixed status system in which there are entrepreneurs, businessmen, capitalists who do what is called "investing for a profit." This whole process is peculiar to a certain type of institutional behavior that has evolved in western civilization. Capitalists invest for a profit and are affected by "uncertainty." It is not the uncertainties of the housewife, or of the Eskimo fishing through the ice, or of a Pueblo Indian rain ceremonial conducted according to priestly guidance, that a classicist such as Professor Robbins has in mind when he speaks of the "universality" of different degrees of uncertainty regarding the future.

All of this discussion of Robbins is to bring out as clearly as possible the fact that the classicist assumes the "natural order" of Adam Smith even when he claims that his economic theory is unrelated to any preconceptions on the naturalness of a particular social order. The order of things that was taking hold in the time of Smith has become imbedded in economic theory, and commercial status groups have become "factors of production" in economic theory. As such, the social origin of these factors is forgotten or obscured, and they are accepted as mechanical components under which all aspects of a complex technological productive-process can be subsumed.

Among classical economists, J. M. Keynes is held to have revolutionized economic theory in his *General Theory of Employment Interest and Money.* In certain respects this is the case, but in certain other respects Keynes' argument is couched in the same terms as that of all the classicists. Keynes' methodology was that of classical economics, using the aggregative approach of Adam Smith with the marginal analysis of the neoclassicist. Throughout the general theory the assumption is always present that economic theory deals with the distribution of income, albeit aggregate income, to the permanent factors, land, labor, and capital. The whole of the *General Theory* is directed to an explanation of the general determinants of employment in a pecuniary economy in which factors of production, land, labor, and capital, are put out for hire by landlord, capitalist, and laborer.

Keynes, like Adam Smith, Ricardo, J. S. Mill, and Marx, holds that the long-term trend is for a falling rate of profit.[28] As he puts it, the marginal efficiency of capital in the long-run

[28] Dudley Dillard, *The Economics of John Maynard Keynes,* New York, Prentice-Hall, 1948, p. 153. J. M. Keynes, *The General Theory of Employment Interest and Money,* New York, Harcourt Brace, 1936, pp. 220-223.

has a tendency to fall toward zero. The tendency, however, brings on the stationary state. But to Keynes, as to all classicists, and unlike Marx, this does not bring in its wake any significant social change. The social structure will remain with only minor alterations and it would serve merely as "the most sensible way of gradually getting rid of many of the objectionable features of capitalism."[29]

To be sure, the fall of the marginal efficiency of capital to zero would result in "the euthenasia of the rentier."[30] To Keynes, "The outstanding faults of the economic society in which we live are its failure to provide for full employment and its arbitrary and inequitable distribution of wealth and incomes."[31] The first problem or fault can be remedied by the program of public policy which follows from Keynes' general theory. The second, Keynes sees being corrected by the present trend toward more steeply graded and all inclusive progressive taxes.[32] To Keynes, capitalist society will continue as it is except for the progressive elimination of the rentier and "a somewhat comprehensive socialisation of investment."[33] Nevertheless, it can be said that the concept of social change is not an integral part of the general theory. Although some find implications in Keynes of a more far-reaching change than Keynes himself saw, Paul Sweezy is substantially correct when he points out that Keynes is true to classical tradition in accepting the classical concept of commercial society as permanent.

> That Keynes held this view was, of course, no accident. He could reject Say's Law and the conclusions based on it, because he thought they were largely responsible for the muddle; but it never occurred to him to question, still less to try to escape from, the broader philosophical and social tradition in which he was reared. The major unspoken premise of that tradition is that capitalism is the only possible form of civilized society.[34]

From Adam Smith to John Maynard Keynes the classicist has always limited his horizon to a social universe consisting of

29 Keynes, *op. cit.*, p. 221.
30 *Ibid.*, pp. 375-376.
31 *Ibid.*, p. 372.
32 *Ibid.*
33 *Ibid.*, p. 378.
34 Paul M. Sweezey, "Keynes, the Economist (3)," reprinted in *The New Economics*, ed. by Seymour Harris, New York, A. Knopf, 1948, p. 106.

landlord, capitalist, and laborer. This is the universe within which price and price movements take place. The market records the sensations of these individuals through price. Change takes place as a consequence of unfulfilled sensations. But this change or action is individual action directed toward a re-establishment of an equilibrium or of mass individual satiation. Action is always on an individual basis within the prescribed social system. The social system is one which results from the individual actions of reasonable men guided by an all-seeing nature.

The Newtonian concept of a fixed stellar universe within which the motion of individually suspended heavenly bodies takes place is paralleled in classical economics by a fixed social framework within which individual human beings move in accordance with the human laws of motion—pleasure and pain. In this concept change is a quantitative and limited change. Change is not viewed as an on-going, all-encompassing process of cumulative changes, but is a sequence of disconnected mechanical actions within a fixed area. This is Newtonian and this aspect of classical economic theory gives to it a Newtonian flavor. It likewise is one of the chief differences between classicism and institutionalism.

Since the development of the concept of culture, man's whole way of viewing society has changed. In the older way, the focus of attention was on men as individuals. Men did things and it was the repetition of "doing things" by men that constituted society. Since the focus of attention was on men, society was held to be merely a collection of men and a discontinuous series of individually calculated actions. This idea of society pervades the economics of the classical economist. Society was nothing more than a set of rules for the guidance of human behavior, these rules having been arrived at by careful calculations and carried out by the exercise of sufficient will. In other words, society was consciously brought into existence by man. Since this is an event which can happen only once, the social order was to all intents and purposes permanent.

This way of viewing society has difficulties. Society could not be distinguished from the individuals who compose it, for it was defined as a collection of individuals. Futile arguments were waged as to which is greater, the society or the individual. To the classicist the answer was clear; since the individual was a segment of society, what was good for that segment was good for society. There are difficulties in this approach that are insurmountable. As we have seen, human behavior is now known to be shaped and conditioned by the cultural milieu.

To the modern social inquirer, man is a social animal. The basic framework of social analysis is now found in culture rather than in individual "human nature." If the forms of behavior in which human action manifests itself are to be explained, they must be explained in terms of culture. Of course this culture is a group phenomenon and of course there are individuals who carry this culture; but human behavior cannot be explained in terms of "will," race, or social interaction.[35]

In modern social inquiry, then, the social nature of human behavior is accepted, but the peculiar characteristics of that behavior must be explained in terms of this superpsychological phenomenon, culture. In other words modern social inquiry makes use of the tool "culture" in observing and analyzing human behavior.

This same human behavior is seen to be subject to a developmental process, a process of cumulative change. Cultures grow and develop, by means of invention and diffusion. The culture trait, the basic unit in culture, is combined with other traits to form what is known as an invention. This invention then diffuses over the culture area and into other culture areas through culture contact. Culture grows and develops by this process of cumulative development and diffusion.[36] Cultural growth is evolutionary, and the very concept of cultural change is Darwinian. Culture develops from the simple to the more complex in a continuous cumulative process. Roland Dixon brings out this point in the introduction to his *The Building of Cultures.*

> Such an analysis of cultures into their component traits enables one not only to compare the cultures qualitatively and quantitatively, but to probe deeply into their origins and manner of growth.

---

35 Leslie White, *The Science of Culture,* pp. 78-79.

36 For discussions of this process see Clark Wissler, *Man and Culture,* New York, Thomas Y. Crowell, 1923; Roland B. Dixon, *The Building of Cultures,* New York, Charles Scribner's Sons, 1928; C. J. Warden, *The Emergence of Human Culture,* New York, Macmillan, 1936.

For as we compare one culture with another, a higher with a lower, the first and most obvious fact which emerges is that the higher cultures differ from the lower in possessing both a greater number of traits as well as traits of a higher stage of development. The wealth of traits which a culture possesses and the stage of perfection of its traits decreases as we descend the scale of culture, until, when we reach such very primitive folk as the now extinct Tasmanians, we are within measurable distance of those very beginnings of culture which set our earliest ancestors off as man.[37]

To the institutional economist economic behavior is cultural behavior, as was indicated in the last chapter. Economic behavior takes place within a cultural milieu and is, in fact, a part of that cultural milieu. In the work of the institutionalist this is of extremely great importance; for he not only explains individual behavior in terms of culture, but he is concerned with economic behavior in general as an aspect of culture. In other words, economic behavior patterns are those aspects of cultural behavior that are concerned with earning a living.

Since the institutionalist conceives society as a cultural phenomenon, the hedonic psychology upon which the classicist based his conception of the social universe is totally rejected. All institutional economists have criticized the classical assumption of a hedonistic calculating human agent. It is now quite apparent even to the superficial observer that man is not such a calculating creature. Folkways and mores prescribe human conduct under given conditions, and these prescriptions form the basis of calculations of pleasure and pain. As Veblen pointed out in his *Theory of the Leisure Class,* some of the most painful habits prevail because they are a part of the institutional fabric. It is this type of behavior that the critics of hedonism have called irrational behavior, insisting that man is not the rational animal of the hedonist.

Recognizing the significance of the cultural milieu, the institutional economist has devoted much time and energy to the study of economic behavior within a larger cultural framework. As one professed institutionalist has stated the case,

Economic activity has little meaning apart from the larger social context in which it takes place. To study the ways by which man

---

[37] Roland B. Dixon, *op. cit.,* p. 4. See also C. J. Warden, *op. cit.,* Chap. IV, "The Evolution of Culture."

satisfies his wants without considering the sources of these wants, the origin of the means employed, and the influence of his beliefs and aspirations, is to study something that does not in reality exist. Man is not a mechanism which can be adjusted to perform first one set of functions and then, with slight readjustment others. He is not engaged at one time in the gaining of a livelihood to the exclusion of his political, social, or religious activities. Instead, his efforts to make a living are directed and conditioned by his whole round of life—his attitudes toward the political organization of his state, toward the other members of his family or club, and toward the church in which he worships. All these in turn are conditioned by his economic activities. Economics is, therefore, not a phase of life but a point of view—a way of studying human activity. To understand modern economic activity, which has become the dominant and directive force in our industrialized world, one must appreciate its place in the social entity called culture.[38]

Because of a realization that economic behavior is cultural in origin and that it cannot be understood when held to be the product of "will" guided by a divinely created "reason," the institutionalist has concerned himself with an understanding of economic institutions. Partly because of this emphasis on the institutional basis of human behavior the institutionalist has been held to claim that human behavior is non-rational.[39] If this has any meaning, it simply means that the institutionalist does not conceive man as a rational being in terms of a hedonistic rationality. To the institutionalist much of the behavior of man within the price system is irrational on the group level. The price system or those patterns of behavior forming the institutional complex known as the price system is, from the viewpoint of Veblen, an irrational or ceremonial pattern of behavior. But more of that later.

To some institutionalists, institutional economics is the study and analysis of economic institutions. This is true of the work of Professor Dixon. Dixon accepts the anthropological approach to culture as outlined in the works of such anthropologists as Clark Wissler and Roland B. Dixon. Culture grows by invention and diffusion. Economic activity is simply a part of

---

38 Russell A. Dixon, *Economic Institutions and Cultural Change*, New York, McGraw-Hill, 1941, p. 5.

39 Lewis H. Haney, *History of Economic Thought*, p. 743.

a larger cultural pattern[40] and is subject to the same process of growth.

According to Professor Dixon economic behavior, like all other behavior, is found organized in complexes or institutions. These institutions are "composed of simpler patterns of behavior called conventions, customs, or folkways."[41] Human behavior is shaped and molded by institutions. "Institutions are created by man but they owe neither their creation nor their existence to any one person."[42] Nevertheless, the behavior of the individual conforms to these institutions.[43]

Although institutional behavior is enforced by social pressure, these patterns of behavior are subject to change. Changes in one part of a culture pattern are ramified throughout the whole pattern. These changes occur through invention and discovery and may have far-reaching consequences for the whole social fabric. This is especially true when the change "appears in the material basis of the social pattern, such as a new technology of production or a revolutionary alteration in the means of transport."[44] Change thus brought about will be resisted by those with a vested interest in the existent institutional framework. Defense will be couched in terms of usage sanctified by ancient prescriptive.

> Such practices may even be endowed with values far removed from the circumstances that gave them birth. The tangled usages and functions are deftly separated from the larger social fabric in which they originally arose. For instance, the price system is traced to a beginning in the natural freedom of man and the tariff to a righteous protection against people of inferior social organization.[45]

According to Dixon, as old institutions are found to be inadequate to deal with problems created by cultural innovation, new institutions are formed that meet the challenge. In other words, social organization is subject to change and new institutions are the result of attempts to meet new problems. Because

---

40 Russell A. Dixon and E. Kingman Eberhart, *Economics and Cultural Change,* New York, McGraw-Hill, 1938, pp. 3 ff.

41 Dixon, *Economic Institutions and Cultural Change,* p. 14.

42 *Ibid.*

43 *Ibid.,* p. 17.

44 *Ibid.,* p. 20.

45 *Ibid.,* p. 21.

of resistance by vested interests these changes are not without some degree of friction.

> The institutions themselves come to be issues while the problems, which only organized action can solve, receive little attention. Thus social change becomes chaotic where it might have been orderly.[46]

On the basis of this general concept of human behavior in which economic behavior is held to be an integral part of total behavior, Dixon undertakes to analyze some basic institutions of modern economic society. This need not detain us here. His work is significant from the standpoint of the present inquiry chiefly because it illustrates the approach of those institutionalists who have taken "institutions" as the basis of economic study.

A far more specialized but similar approach is to be found in the Berle and Means study of the modern corporation.[47] To Berle and Means "the modern corporation may be regarded not simply as one form of social organization but potentially (if not actually) as the dominant institution of the modern world."[48] Traditional economic theory is inadequate to explain the role of the modern corporation in present-day society. Adam Smith envisaged an economic universe inhabited by individual enterprisers who owned and controlled their own property unit. But the modern corporation has completely altered the institution of property. Property no longer is something tangible controlled by the individual who holds title to the property. Ownership in the modern corporation has become only a claim on a portion of the pecuniary earning power of that corporation. The corporation must be studied as a social organization or institution.[49]

It was to just such an analysis that Berle and Means subjected the modern corporation. Unlike the traditional price theorist who fits the corporation into his hedonistic theory under the heading, "The Economics of the Firm," and goes on to treat it as subject to the same hedonic calculations that he assumes explain individual behavior, Berle and Means treat the corporation, its growth and structural changes, as part of the institutional fabric of modern society. A large part of the study

46 *Ibid.*, p. 22.

47 Adolph A. Berle, Jr. and Gardiner C. Means, *The Modern Corporation and Private Property*, New York, Macmillan, 1932.

48 *Ibid.*, p. 356.

49 *Ibid.*, pp. 352-353.

is devoted to a detailed analysis of how this institutional fabric has been changing through growth and new usage.[50]

On a broader plain, John R. Commons also treated economic phenomena as "collective action" and as subject to change. Commons held that the classical economists had continually confused capital as material and capital as pecuniary value imputed to ownership. As a consequence they failed to understand that it was ownership that was exchanged in the market and not the physical property.[51] They took this exchange as the basis for study.[52]

Commons takes the transaction as the basic economic unit. A transaction is a transfer of future ownership and all of the rights of future ownership of future things.[53] In Commons' analysis there are three types of transactions: (1) bargaining transactions which take place between buyers and sellers, (2) the managerial transactions which take place between legal superior and legal inferior, and (3) rationing transactions which "differ from Bargaining and Managing Transactions in that they are the negotiations of reaching an agreement among several participants who have authority to apportion the benefits and burdens to members of a joint enterprise."[54]

According to Commons, "These three types of transactions are brought together in a larger unit of economic investigation . . . named a Going Concern."[55] Going concerns are such things as "the family, the corporation, the trade association," and even the state itself. Passively these going concerns are known as "the group" and actively as the "going concern." Each is governed by a set of working rules which prescribe and proscribe certain types of human behavior.[56] In other words, all activity is collective activity which takes place within the working rules that govern the behavior of those within a going concern.

Despite the peculiar terminology used by Commons it is

[50] *Ibid.*, Book II, "Regrouping of Rights: Relative Legal Position of Ownership and Control," pp. 127-287.

[51] John R. Commons, *Institutional Economics*, New York, Macmillan, 1934, p. 55.

[52] *Ibid.*, p. 56.

[53] *Ibid.*, p. 58.

[54] *Ibid.*, pp. 67-68.

[55] *Ibid.*, p. 69.

[56] *Ibid.*, pp. 70-71.

clear that he is in general agreement with those institutionalists who place great emphasis on the institutional basis of human behavior. He places the usual emphasis on the role of custom in shaping human behavior,[57] and his use of going concern is related in his own work to what is commonly meant by institution. What he calls working rules governing the behavior of going concerns are similar to the folkways and mores as used by other institutional economists. Throughout his work, Commons likewise places much emphasis on "perpetual change which is the uncertain future world of institutional economics."[58] In other words "going concerns" (institutions) and "working rules" (folkways and mores) are subject to continual change. Social structure to Commons is not fixed for all eternity. This aspect of his system would place Commons in the institutionalist camp.

Those institutional economists reviewed thus far have one thing in common—that is, their emphasis on custom and habit in shaping collective behavior. The social framework, within which economic activity takes place, shapes and molds that economic activity. In other words, economic behavior is looked upon as institutionally conditioned behavior. But the most important common point of agreement of all of these institutionalists is that institutions are modes of social organization. They represent a way of order. These modes of organization are subject to change as man faces new problems and new needs. They are, therefore, in a constant state of change. Although all institutionalists have emphasized the importance of change to economic theory and most have alluded to evolution, those who have concentrated their attention on the institution have not developed an explicitly evolutionary economics. Change is not something that is characteristic of the system itself. Change is something cataclysmic from without the system. That is, unlike the evolutionary point of view of Darwinism, change is held to be separate from the system itself which forces an institutional readjustment.

These economists have begun their economic inquiry with a concept of an institution somewhat as described by Walton Hamilton.

---

[57] *Ibid.*, pp. 50-51, 80.
[58] *Ibid.*, p. 93.

> Institution is a verbal symbol which for want of a better describes a cluster of social usages. It connotes a way of thought or action of some prevalence and permanence which is imbedded in the habits of a group or the customs of a people. In ordinary speech it is another word for procedure, convention, or arrangement; in the language of books it is the singular of which the mores or the folkways are the plural. Institutions fix the confines of and impose form upon the activities of human beings. The world of use and wont, to which imperfectly we accomodate our lives, is a tangled unbroken web of institutions.[59]

Under this definition or description the "range of institutions is as wide as the interests of mankind."[60] All human behavior becomes subsumed under some institution so that such diverse things as "barter, burial, worship, the dietary, the work life, the sex union" are all institutions as well as "that body of ideas taken for granted which is called common sense"[61] and "the way of knowledge."[62] Professor Dixon uses a similarly all-inclusive definition when he includes among modern institutions, science and technology.[63]

This use of institution and the resulting view of society, leaves society a stable and yet an unstable thing. Since institutions have the authentication of custom and habit or usage they are relatively stable. On the other hand, the institutional structure is subject to constant alteration because of cataclysmic change from without the institutional framework. In other words, the dynamic process of change is left out of the system. This is reminiscent to a certain extent of the classicist's concept of change, the important difference being that the classicist foresees no continuing change in social organization. The history of mankind is a trail of wrecked institutions that have been replaced by new ones, only to meet the same fate.

> In the ceaseless course of human events a countless number of systems under which the material resources of society are ordered have emerged, had their brief day and passed. In the making of these deliberate intent has had its part, as when a Tudor England promulgated a statute of apprentices or a mercantile United States

---

[59] Walton H. Hamilton, "Institutions," *Encyclopedia of the Social Sciences*, New York, Macmillan, 1932, Vol. 8, p. 84.
[60] *Loc. cit.*
[61] *Ibid.*, p. 85.
[62] *Ibid.*, p. 88.
[63] Dixon, *Economic Institutions and Cultural Change*, pp. 269-327.

invoked an industrial recovery act; but for the most part they have just grown.[64]

Since the economic organization is subject to disrupting influences that bring on constant reorganization, the best that man can hope to do is to use intelligence in guiding this change.

It [economic organization] is not a separate and distinct thing, like a square or a checkerboard, that has a jurisdiction and a law all its own. Instead it is an aspect of all life and all culture. There was a time when students spoke convincingly about keeping the existing order or hopefully about establishing a new one. But the system which the timid would keep has already gone; and the utopia of the reckless is not to be had through a single heroic act of creation. All that a people can do is to shape as intelligently as they can a change which is inevitable.[65]

This type of approach results in a chronicling of successive institutional patterns and lends some credence to critics of institutionalism who have claimed that the institutionalists have contributed nothing new to economic methodology that was not contributed by the Historical School and that they have produced nothing but some "worthwhile descriptive studies . . . embodied in monographs."[66]

At this point, however, other institutionalists have posed two questions. First, is this all that can be said about social organization? That is, is social organization nothing but customarily sanctioned behavior? Or is there another aspect to human behavior that has been overlooked? According to the classicists, the institutionalist looks upon human behavior as irrational; and this criticism is just if there is nothing more to be said about social organization. Secondly, it might be asked, has institutionalism nothing more to offer? Have all institutionalists stopped at "institutions" in their economic inquiry? If the answer to both of these questions is in the affirmative, then it can hardly be contended that the institutionalist has developed an evolutionary or Darwinian view of society. Certainly his concept of social organization differs from that of the classicist. No institutionalist holds to a social order fixed for all eternity. But to those who have focused attention on institutions, change is not ac-

64 Walton Hamilton, "Organization, Economic," *Encyclopedia of the Social Sciences,* Vol. XI, p. 485.

65 *Ibid.,* pp. 489-490.

66 Lewis Haney, *op. cit.,* p. 748.

counted for in evolutionary terms. Change is spasmodic and cataclysmic, bringing on the demise of old habits and usages and the creation of new.

But this by no means is all that can be said about social organization nor is it all that the institutionalists have to offer on the subject. There is a hint of something else in one of Hamilton's articles. He seems to make a distinction between workaday tasks based on matter-of-fact and other, more distinctively ceremonial, behavior, but he does not develop the idea.

> In the ordinary ways of winning from the environment a precarious living—the gathering of fruits, the stalking of game, the tilling of soil—there is a great ceremonial, which envelopes technology in routine and magic and is a worship, a government and a mode of tribal life as well as a rule for industry.[67]

In his *Economics of Collective Action,* Commons in several places came remarkably near the distinction between institution and technology that lay at the foundation of the work of Veblen. He made a distinction between wealth and asset and between man-hour efficiency and dollar efficiency.[68] He noted that business efficiency and engineering efficiency are distinct and not identical as the classical economists assumed. However, he is not as explicit as Veblen in claiming that business efficiency undermines engineering efficiency. Commons saw faintly the difference between the technological aspects of the life process and the ceremonial as manifested in our integrated technical structure and our complex credit structure. But, unlike Veblen, he does not follow this up by showing the nature of the credit structure as contrasted with the industrial structure nor the role of the credit structure as a permissive agent at best and a disruptive one at worst. He did recognize the disruptive character at times. Nevertheless, he demonstrates throughout the volume an awareness of the technological and ceremonial patterns of culture as revealed in modern society.[69] Although neither Hamilton nor Commons developed this kernel of an idea any further, Veblen and other institutionalists have done so.

Veblen was a close student of the anthropology of his day, and he borrowed freely from the concepts of the anthropologist.

---

67 Hamilton, "Organization, Economic," p. 485.
68 Commons, *Economics of Collective Action,* pp. 94-95, 100-101.
69 *Ibid.*, pp. 44-46, 48, 53, 84, 229-230.

In order fully to understand Veblen's concepts of social organization, it is expedient to stop for a moment and look into the findings of the anthropologists on social organization.

One thing that the anthropologists have found is the widespread existence of magic among primitive peoples. Brute force is looked upon as spiritually motivated, and animism and anthropomorphism are widespread. This attitude or outlook results in elaborate ceremonials aimed at placating the spirits and giving to the occurrence of every day events a certain "ceremonial adequacy." This aspect of primitive society cannot fail to be observed for it is the dramatic aspect of what otherwise may be a very routine yet precarious existence. Thus in all cultural anthropology much time is devoted to the elaboration of magic, myth, and ceremony, or to the institutional fabric of that society.

But this is not by any means all that can be found in primitive society. All primitives have a rather large accumulation of matter-of-fact information, the product of careful observation of action and consequence. In fact no group could continue to exist without this store of accumulated and empirically authenticated information. They know how to kindle a fire, what type of sapling is best for the construction of a bow, how to bend and shape bamboo for the construction of a shelter, and which berries and plants are edible and which are poisonous. Every group has a large accumulation of this type of information upon which it is absolutely dependent for a livelihood. Yet in the behavior of the group these two types of knowledge, myth and matter-of-fact, are blended in patterns composed of an element of each. Malinowski in speaking of this aspect of the behavior of the Trobriand Islanders, makes the phenomenon especially clear.

As the Melanisians are reputed, however, to be specially magic-ridden, they will furnish an acid test of the existence of empirical and rational knowledge among savages living in the age of polished stone.

These natives, and I am speaking mainly of the Melanisians who inhabit the coral atolls to the N. E. of the main island, the Trobriand Archipelago and the adjoining groups, are expert fishermen, industrious manufacturers and traders, but they rely mainly on gardening for their existence. With the most rudimentary implements, a pointed digging-stick and a small axe, they are able to raise crops sufficient to maintain a dense population and even yielding a surplus, which in olden days was allowed to rot unconcerned, and which at present is exported to feed plantation hands. The success in their agriculture depends—besides the excellent natural conditions with which they are favored—upon their extensive knowledge of the classes of the soil, of the various cultivated plants, of the mutual adaptation of these two factors, and, last not least, upon their knowledge of the importance of accurate hard work. They have to select the soil and the seedlings, they have appropriately to fix the times for clearing and burning the scrub, for planting and weeding, for training the vines of the yam-plants. In all this they are guided by a clear knowledge of weather and seasons, plants and pests, soil and tubers, and by a conviction that this knowledge is true and reliable, that it can be counted upon and must be scrupulously obeyed.

Yet mixed with all their activities there is to be found magic, a series of rites performed every year over the gardens in rigorous sequence and order. Since the leadership in garden work is in the hands of the magician, and since ritual and practical work are intimately associated, a superficial observer might be led to assume that the mystic and the material behavior are mixed up, that their effects are not distinguished by the natives and not distinguishable in scientific analysis. Is this so really?

Magic is undoubtedly regarded by the natives as absolutely indispensable to the welfare of the gardens. What would happen without it no one can exactly tell, for no native garden has ever been made without its ritual, in spite of some thirty years of European rule and missionary influence and well over a century's contact with white traders. But certainly various kinds of disaster, blight, unseasonable droughts and rains, wild-pigs and locusts, would destroy the unhallowed garden made without magic.

Does this mean, however, that the natives attribute all the good results to magic? Certainly not. If you were to suggest to a native that he should make his garden mainly by magic and scamp his work, he would simply smile on your simplicity.[70]

These two aspects of human culture have been widely noted by anthropologists and archaeologists. It is this phenomenon in human culture of which Veblen and his followers make much use.[71]

In all societies there is found both magic-and-myth and matter of fact. This blending, however, affects the whole social

---

70 Bronislaw Malinowski, *Magic, Science and Religion,* Glencoe, Ill., The Free Press, 1948, pp. 10-11.

71 Thorstein Veblen, *The Place of Science in Modern Civilization,* p. 8, pp. 40-46, pp. 62-64; *Imperial Germany and the Industrial Revolution,* pp. 19-43; *The Instinct of Workmanship,* Chap. II.

organization. Veblen's concept of social organization is closely related to his psychological concepts, which were treated in the last chapter. In his system social organization can be broken down into institutional patterns and instrumental or technological patterns of behavior. These social patterns are reflections of the habits of thought of the community which in turn reflect the habits of life. Behavior of a ceremonial or institutional character is subject to check or authentication by the test of dramatic consistency.[72] These patterns of behavior are coercive in nature, being enforced by social pressure in different form and degree on the different classes of the community.[73] Such patterns are closely tied to matters of rank and status and are essentially conservative in nature, for they are looked upon as of the greatest importance to the welfare of the group.[74]

Ceremonial behavior, of a "magical, or religious, conventional, or pecuniary nature" is to be found closely allied with technological behavior. Veblen's idea of the relationship between these two is similar to that illustrated in a passage by Gordon Childe showing the same relationship in the copper age.

> Metallurgical lore is the first approximation to international science. But it remains craft lore. All the practical science of the ancient smiths and miners was certainly embedded in an unpractical matrix of magic ritual. Assyrian texts, even in the First Millenium B. C., contain hints of what such rituals may have involved—foetuses and virgin's blood. So do the remains of a bronze-workers' encampment in Heathery Burn Cave (Co. Durham) in England. Today barbarian smiths' operations are surrounded with a complex of magical precautions.[75]

Veblen calls attention to this same phenomenon in the following passage:

> In many of the lower cultures, or perhaps rather in such of the lower cultures as are at all well known, the workday routine of getting a living is encumbered with a ubiquitous and pervasive scheme of such magical or superstitious conceits and observances, which are felt to constitute an indispensable part of the industrial processes in which they mingle. They embody the putatively efficacious immaterial constituent of all technological procedure; or, seen in detail, they are the spiritual half that completes and animates

72 Veblen, *The Place of Science*, pp. 41-44.

73 *Ibid.*, pp. 44-45.

74 Veblen, *Imperial Germany*, pp. 25-26.

75 V. Gordon Childe, *What Happened in History*, New York, Penguin Books, (New American Library), 1946, p. 71.

any process or device throughout its participation in the industrial routine. Like the technological elements with which they are associated, and concomitantly with them, these magically efficacious devices have grown into the prevalent habits of thought of the population and have become an integral part of the common-sense notion of how these technological elements are and are to be turned to account. And at a slightly farther shift in the current of sophistication, out of the same penchant for anthropomorphic interpretation and analogy, a wide range of religious observances, properly so called, will also presently come to bear on the industrial process and the routine of economic life; with a proliferous growth of ceremonial; of propitiation and avoidance, designed to further the propitious course of things to be done.[76]

But this dichotomy is not limited to primitive peoples. The notable contribution of Veblen was that he brought to bear on present day culture the tools of analysis that the anthropologist found so fruitful in the inquiry into primitive society. No society believes that it believes in magic. Taken at its face value as presented by the keepers of a particular culture, magic does not appear as such in that culture. Every aspect of the cultural fabric has some purpose; if not empirically demonstrable, it is in that realm of things put safely beyond the necessity for empirical verification. The truth of the latter is a matter of common sense or is vouched for by authority. The fact that Veblen saw this dichotomy not as a part of primitive society alone, but as a part of all societies, makes his use of the methods of the anthropologist significant.

According to Veblen, all culture is characterized by this combination of magic or ceremonial and technological behavior. That is precisely the significance of *The Theory of the Leisure Class*. Certainly Veblen did not mean to write a hilariously amusing work pointing out some of the more absurd punctilios of dress and eating. What *The Theory of the Leisure Class* clearly points out is the ceremonial aspect of eating, dressing, educating, entertaining, etc. Nor was *The Theory of Business Enterprise* conceived solely as a polemic against the business man; nor was *The Engineers and the Price System* written solely to eulogize the engineer. Such may have been some of the effects of these books; but surely it is clear that Veblen was pointing out those aspects of contemporary culture

[76] Veblen, *Imperial Germany*, pp. 26-27.

that are ceremonial in nature and those that are instrumental or technological.

Once this distinction is clearly seen, the seeming enigma of the dynamic and static aspects of culture becomes clear. Culture is made up of dynamic and static elements that appear "in some sort of symbiosis."[77] Veblen and other institutional economists call the static element institutions; the dynamic element is called technology. Both are patterns of behavior. The two are found in a "symbiotic" relationship.[78]

What makes institutions static is the fact that the ultimate test of authenticity for any institutional pattern rests on authority—the authority of magic, religion, habit, and custom reinforced by a mythical efficacy. The institutional pattern is tied closely to the system of status of the community to which is attributed great significance. All groups have been graded into positions of higher and lower status in accordance with an imputed efficacy to perform feats of prowess, whether religious, military, pecuniary, or scientific. Certainly in our own culture theories of value, such as the labor theory of value, and theories of income distribution, such as marginal productivity, are elaborate scholastic attempts to give a rational authentication to an already established difference that seems of the greatest importance to the institutionally conditioned group.

From this ceremonial point of view no physical force, not even that of man, is looked upon in matter-of-fact terms. People engaged in physical activities are seen as performing feats of prowess, of manhandling the brute forces of nature by means of chicane and clever deceit. It is to intercessions of the priest that man must look to explain an abundant crop.[79] It is by legally valid manipulations of corporate securities and by the gracious permission of accumulated wealth that the unprecedented output of modern industry is explained. That is what is meant by the necessity for preserving "business venture" and "risk capital." Anyone can raise crops and anyone can make steel, but not just anyone can perform these higher acts which give to the production of crops and steel their ceremonial adequacy.

---

77 Veblen, *Imperial Germany*, p. 37.

78 C. E. Ayres, "The Coordinates of Institutionalism," *The American Economic Review*, Vol. XLI, No. 2, May 1951, p. 51.

79 Veblen, *The Instinct of Workmanship*, pp. 155-156.

Thus, it comes about that there are various roles in society which give to those fulfilling them a particular status within the institutional framework. These status positions are defined by mores which prescribe what is construed to be appropriate behavior within any given role.[80] Such mores define status-relationships within the institutional fabric. The whole process is justified by myth and has the authentication of the ancestors.[81] As such it is not subject to empirical verification and is believed to be true beyond the necessity of further inquiry. In fact inquiry would be impertinent. This supposition gives to the ceremonial behavior pattern its peculiar rigidity. Hence it is the rigid aspect of culture.[82]

But this is by no means all there is to culture. Of course, it is a significant part of culture, for it influences and puts a brake on technological development. On the other hand, a large part of culture is made up of matter-of-fact knowledge and behavior of just the kind described by Malinowski. It is these patterns of behavior that have been neglected by those students of culture who have been more concerned with the dramatic aspects of human culture.[83] When the cultural anthropologist speaks of the instability of culture and its tendency to grow, it is the technological aspect that he has in view. For it is the nature of technology to grow and expand. Technology, or patterns of tool using, expand by a process of cumulative growth.[84] This accumulation comes about by the combination of old traits into new. Thus the automobile is the combination of the carriage and the internal combustion engine.

It is this aspect of culture that the institutionalist has in mind when he speaks of developing an evolutionary economics. Traditionally this process has been thought to be beyond the limits of economic inquiry, as the classicist has focused his attention on that more dramatic institutional fabric, the price system. Yet the technological aspect of western culture is held by the institutionalist to be its dynamic aspect.

To some, this seems to be utter nonsense, for they claim that "tools are neutral." Tools are nothing without men. To

---

80 C. E. Ayres, *The Theory of Economic Progress,* pp. 163-164.
81 *Ibid.,* pp. 170-172.
82 *Ibid.,* pp. 174-176.
83 Veblen, *The Place of Science,* p. 43
84 Ayres, *op. cit.,* pp. 119-123.

this the institutionalist makes two replies. First, technology is of course carried along by the activities of men, but these men are part of a cultural scheme that includes technological elements. As Veblen put it,

> Technological knowledge is of the nature of a common stock, held and carried forward collectively by the community, which is in this relation to be conceived as a going concern. The state of the industrial arts is a fact of group life, not of individual or private initiative or innovation. It is an affair of the collectivity, not a creative achievement of individuals working self-sufficiently in severalty or in isolation.[85]

Second, technology does not imply tools without the related social uses of these tools. In other words, technology is not the accumulation of "tools for tools' sake." These tools are an integral part of behavior patterns that are interrelated in the on-going life process. To Veblen as to all institutionalists, technology has a different meaning from that accorded it in common usage.[86] Tools imply use. A spade implies digging and gardening; an oven implies heating processes such as cooking, pottery making, metal smelting; and both of these imply all of the related organizational patterns of behavior incorporated in the use of these tools. But technology, since it is dynamic, implies a continued growth and more complex development in human culture. The test of adequacy for technology is a matter-of-fact test of its ability to accomplish a particular end-in-view. This being the case, it is open to development and growth.

This does not mean to imply that the institutionalist holds that technology is always free to expand and grow. Technology is but one part of an integrated cultural whole of which ceremonialism is the other aspect. The institutionalist holds that this ceremonialism may be inhibitory. Veblen made much of this fact. In his *Theory of Business Enterprise* he went to great lengths to show that the activities and habits of thought engendered by business were at variance with the habits and attitudes engendered by the machine process.[87] The result was

---

85 Veblen, *The Instinct of Workmanship*, p. 103.

86 Veblen, *The Place of Science*, p. 16.

87 Veblen, *The Theory of Business Enterprise*, New York, Charles Scribner's Sons, 1935, Chap. IV; see also *The Engineers and the Price System*, New York, Viking, 1947, Chap. I.

a regular and "conscientious withdrawal of efficiency." He accounted for the technological advances of Germany over England by the fact that Germany borrowed the modern industrial technology from England without the related ceremonial encumbrances.[88] Likewise, England was able earlier to make great strides in the development of technology because of her relative freedom from the predatory adventures of the dynastic states on the continent. The lowland countries, from whom the English borrowed, were constantly disrupted and preoccupied by these ventures in kingly and patriotic aggrandizement.[89] Thus, the institutional fabric may be of such a rigid nature as to stifle completely any technological advance. This accounts for the long periods of time during which some cultures have remained dormant.

On the other hand, the institutionalist also holds that technology erodes the institutional aspect of culture. That is what Veblen means when he states that "modern civilization is peculiarly matter-of-fact."[90] The inroads made upon habitual thought by the advance of modern technology have made for a significantly matter-of-fact outlook. New technology is disruptive of old institutionalized patterns of behavior. It is modern technology that is breaking up the old homestead-family, not a disappearance of "moral fiber."[91] Nor is the problem one of creating new institutions. Institutions to the institutionalist are not replaced, but somewhat like old soldiers, "they just fade away!" As Veblen so aptly stated it,

> If there is anywhere a safe negative conclusion, it is that an institution grown mischievous by obsolescence need not be replaced by a substitute.
>
> Instances of such mischievous institutional arrangements, obsolete or in process of obsolescence, would be, e. g., the French monarchy of the ancient regime, the Spanish Inquisition, the British corn laws and the "rotten boroughs," the Barbary pirates, the Turkish rule in Armenia, the British crown, the German Imperial Dynasty, the European balance of powers, the Monroe Doctrine. In some sense, at least in the sense and degree implied in their selective survival, these various articles of institutional furniture,

88 Veblen, *Imperial Germany,* Chap. VI.

89 Veblen, *The Instinct of Workmanship,* pp. 246-251.

90 Veblen, *The Place of Science,* p. 1.

91 C. E. Ayres, *Science, the False Messiah,* Indianapolis, Bobbs-Merrill, 1927, Chap. VIII.

and many like them, have once presumably been suitable to some end, in the days of their origin and vigorous growth; and they have at least in some passable fashion met some felt want; but if they ever had a place and use in human economy they have in time grown imbecile and mischievous by force of changing circumstances, and the question is not how to replace them with something else to the same purpose after their purpose is outworn. A man who loses a wart off the end of his nose does not apply to the *Ersatz* bureau for a convenient substitute.[92]

Growth and development through technological process take place in culture when the institutional framework is not such as to stifle that growth completely. Where growth is possible, the technological development will erode the institutional encumbrances.

To the institutionalist, the present-day economic culture is dominated by business enterprise and the machine technology.[93] The advance of the machine technology has made significant inroads on business enterprise. The importance of Berle and Mean's study is that they demonstrate the extent to which the institution of ownership has already been eroded. The institutionalist by no means holds that things are unfolding in the direction of some transcendental end. Whether technology will continue to develop or whether it will be overcome by "imbecile institutions" remains to be seen.[94]

Taking culture as the basic framework for economic inquiry, the institutionalists, such as Veblen and Ayres and to a lesser extent Commons, have found a dynamic force in technology and a static element in institutions. Their concept of cultural growth is said to be Darwinian because of the technological nature of cultural growth. Veblen held that classical political economy was pre-Darwinian because in its concentration on the ceremonial aspect of culture it failed to develop an evolutionary economics.[95]

Institutional economics can be contrasted with that of the classicists in terms of the concept of social organization. The institutionalist has focused his attention on culture, a concept, or tool of analysis, that developed after the major framework

92 Veblen, *The Nature of Peace,* New York, Viking Press, 1945, p. 216.
93 Veblen, *The Theory of Business Enterprise,* p. 1.
94 *Ibid.,* pp. 399-400; C. E. Ayres, *The Theory of Economic Progress,* p. 176.
95 Veblen, *The Place of Science,* p. 59.

of classical political economy had been established. Some institutionalists such as Professor Dixon and Walton Hamilton have not made a clear-cut distinction between the ceremonial and technological aspects of culture. Nevertheless, all have been impressed by the importance of technology, a factor which the classicist has taken as not worthy of serious consideration. Taking the industrial arts for granted, the classicist has concerned himself with developing a rational explanation for the set of behavior patterns that are involved in the modern institutional galaxy, enterprise, property, ownership, and the price system.

The economic theory of the classicist has been worked out within a fixed social framework which is not subject to change as it is a part of the status system associated with the price system. Since the classicist has concerned himself with "rationalizing" this ceremonial aspect of culture, he has not developed an evolutionary concept of social organization, for ceremonial behavior is essentially static. On this ground, then, it is proper to call the classicist pre-Darwinian. To the extent that he accepts this ceremonial aspect of culture as a part of a larger whole, the "natural order," his concept of social organization is essentially "Newtonian." What change does take place occurs within a fixed and natural order. It is mechanical change.

On the other hand, all institutionalists, starting with culture, look upon the social order as a changing thing, but one that is subject to an evolutionary process of cumulative change. Culture is held to be dynamic and to grow by trait combination. But the part of culture that grows by such a process is that which some institutionalists have called technology. Veblen and those institutionalists who have been close followers of his lead hold that this advance in technology when uninhibited by institutional proscription is erosive of the institutional aspect. Thus culture grows in complexity by trait combination, through an evolutionary process of cumulative growth from simple to more complex forms. In this sense the institutionalist theory of social organization is Darwinian. Nothing is fixed; there is cumulative growth; and there is no transcendental end toward which the process is oriented. Such is the nature of Darwinism.

V

CHANGE AND PROGRESS

It remains to compare the classical and institutionalist theories of progress. Progress has been given a bad name in recent social thought, largely because of the popularity of the "mores-nihilism" of cultural relativism. In fact, it has been in an attempt to escape from the critics of progress that the classical economists have fled to a seemingly safe position by proclaiming that "equilibrium is just equilibrium." Nevertheless, as one writer has stated, "Economic thinking has always embodied some conception of progress and must always do so; for the concept of value is the chief concern of economic thinking, and progress is indissociable from value."[1] Although the contemporary classicist may claim that his theory is free of value connotations, classical theory has always, at least implicitly, contained a theory of progress. Kenneth Boulding is explicit in asserting the necessity for a theory of progress when he states that, "The equilibrium concept is not, therefore, a sufficient guide in the criticism of economic systems or policies; it must be supplemented by some theory of economic progress."[2] Although some classicists shy away from dealing with progress directly, Boulding presents in brief compass the classical doctrine of economic progress, without any equivocation or misgivings.

All classicists center their theories of progress in what is called the process of capital formation. Boulding follows the usual procedure. Progress is identical with improvement in the means of production. Although there may be some question as to what economic progress is, it is true that,

> In some sense all would agree that the replacement of the candle by the kerosene lamp, of the kerosene lamp by the gas mantle, and of the gas mantle by the electric bulb, represent economic progress. Similarly, the chain that leads from the ox cart to the truck, or from the sedan chair to the automobile, or from the hoe to the cultivator, or from the sickle to the combine-harvester likewise represent economic progress.[3]

---

[1] C. E. Ayres, *The Theory of Economic Progress,* p. 231.
[2] Kenneth Boulding, *Economic Analysis,* p. 646.
[3] *Ibid.,* p. 646.

Like all contemporary classicists, Boulding assumes the duality of ends-means; and he therefore assumes that there is more to be said about economic progress than at first meets the eye. "It is evident that economic progress is something real; it is also evident that it is not the whole story."[4] Economic progress increases the power of the means to achieve given ends, but it says nothing about the ends. An end is "not within the province of economic analysis; indeed, it lies in the domain of wisdom rather than knowledge, of religion rather than of science."[5] This separation of ends and means is characteristic of classical political economy. Boulding comments that despite all of the technological advance of the past few centuries, modern man does not come off well when compared culturally, morally, and esthetically with his predecessors. This is the same position as that taken one hundred years ago by John Stuart Mill in his *Principles*.[6]

This separation of the technological from the "cultural or moral" life is a reflection of the conception of society held by the classicists. Life seemed to them a discontinuous thing, a series of consummatory ends, each independent of the other. These ends are absolute and are beyond scientific inquiry and, as Boulding so typically contends, must be left to that time-tested keeper of wisdom, the theologian. As will be shown later, this position differs markedly from that of the institutionalist and makes for a considerable difference in their theories of progress. It also leads the classicist to a depreciation of technological advance as he seeks an explanation of progress in more dramatic aspects of culture.

Since Boulding holds, as do all classicists, that economic progress is a matter of improving "means," the question he seeks to answer is, how are "means" improved? What accounts for more efficient means? The answer to this question is found in the process of capital formation.

From the time of Adam Smith at least, the classicist has tied progress to what he calls "capital accumulation." Capital is defined as "produced means for further production" and

---

[4] *Ibid.*, p. 647.
[5] *Ibid.*
[6] J. S. Mill, *Principles of Political Economy*, p. 751.

progress is held to be the result of increasing these produced means. A greater output of goods and services will result from increased means of production and living standards will be raised. But it is at this point of the argument that a shift in the meaning of capital takes place which makes considerable difference in the results, as will be seen. Capital, defined as "produced means of further production," supposedly means technological knowledge and implements of production. Thus it is by increasing this fund of knowledge and stock of tools that progress is assured. But how is this increase procured?

Professor Boulding, like all classicists, has a ready answer. Capital is increased by accumulation and "The rate of technical progress, therefore, is limited by the conditions which limit the rate of accumulation of capital."[7]

Since accumulation "is the excess of production over consumption," accumulation is the result of not consuming. In other words, capital—meaning tools, implements, and techniques—is accumulated by means of a tightening of the belt, or by means of "abstaining" from consuming. This, he says,

> explains the great difficulty experienced by any poor society in making progress; the degree of "abstinence" (i. e., restriction of consumption) necessary for accumulation represents a disutility greater than can be endured. Below a certain critical point, therefore, the level of which depends of course on the character of the people and the society concerned, progress is impossible. The society treads an endless treadmill of poverty; low production makes it impossible to accumulate, and without accumulation there can be no increase in production.[8]

Nevertheless, there is no reason to assume that a poor society must always remain in such dire straights. Boulding is reassuring on this doubt for, as he states, "once a certain critical point has been passed, progress becomes almost inevitable."[9] Once a society has found it possible to accumulate, further accumulation becomes easier. Exactly how this "critical point" is passed he does not explain. Thus Professor Boulding makes no improvement on the theory of capital accumulation left by

7 Boulding, *op. cit.*, p. 654.
8 *Ibid.*, p. 655.
9 *Ibid.*

Böhm-Bawerk.[10] For Boulding, as for Böhm-Bawerk, progress is identical with tightening one's belt.

Most contemporary classicists do not leave the argument at this point, as it is too absurd for serious consideration. Most but use this theory of primitive accumulation to embellish their more serious argument that capital is accumulated in a monetary society by saving. They identify non-consuming with saving. Since it is money funds that are saved, capital accumulation and progress are tied to the enhancement of pecuniary values. By some feat of magic money funds become the tools, machines, and techniques of production. A mystic potency is imputed to money funds.

This aspect of classical political economy has been noted by many writers.[11] But it merits notice here since it goes a long way to explain the classicist's concern with the institutional rubric of the economic process, the price system. Since progress is identified with the accumulation of money funds, the price system is indeed of great significance for the welfare of mankind. This is so because it is through the price system that pecuniary funds are accumulated. Pecuniary accumulation is possible because of the differential price placed upon one occupation as against another on the basis of a putative production differential. Thus, pecuniary accumulation is tied to the system of status as it manifests itself in the price system. Since the classicist has concentrated his attention on the pecuniary aspect of culture, he has identified progress with the enhanced putative pecuniary worth of ownership claims. Progress is merely a quantitative increase of pecuniary values. No other social change is anticipated.

Thus progress becomes identified with capitalism. The price system is a cultural phenomenon peculiar in its all-pervading nature to capitalism. It is in capitalism that "saving" is reputed to be such an important phenomenon. Most classicists hold that progress and capitalism are not only compatible, but that capitalism acts as a catalytic agent in securing progress. Al-

---

10 Böhm-Bawerk, *The Positive Theory of Capital,* Book II, Chaps. IV, V.

11 See for instance, C. E. Ayres, *The Divine Right of Capital,* Boston, Houghton Mifflin, 1946, pp. 5-6.

though many would not agree with the blatant extremism of Joseph Schumpeter, the statement that follows is typical of the more intense eulogies.

> And now we are at long last face to face with the immediate goal to which that complex yet inadequate argument was to lead. Not only the modern mechanical plant and the volume of the output that pours forth from it, not only modern technology and economic organization, but all the features and achievements of modern capitalism are, directly or indirectly, the products of the capitalist process. They must be included in any balance sheet of it and in any verdict about its deeds or misdeeds.
>
> There is the growth of rational science and the long list of its applications. Airplanes, refrigerators, television, and that sort of thing are immediately recognizable as results of the profit economy. But although the modern hospital is not as a rule operated for profit, it is nonetheless the product of capitalism not only, to repeat, because the capitalist process supplies the means and the will, but much more fundamentally because capitalist rationality supplied the habits of mind that evolved the methods used in these hospitals. And the victories, not yet completely won but in the offing, over cancer, syphilis, and tuberculosis will be as much capitalist achievements as motorcars or pipe lines or Bessemer steel have been.[12]

Although, as previously pointed out, not many classicists would make such sweeping statements, certainly most would be willing to go along with Professor Boulding in emphasizing the failure of socialism to assure progress.

> The hope which many once saw in socialism is now seen to be an illusion. We cannot abolish poverty by passing legislation or by a mere redistribution of wealth. The attempt to redistribute income often destroys it, and there seems to be a certain inexorability about the laws of supply which exacts retribution from the optimistic reformer. If, for instance, society is not willing to pay for the scarce and expensive service of entrepreneurs, those services will not be forthcoming. A large part of the failure of the Russian experiment may be due to this factor, for the destruction of the private entrepreneur and the kulak in Russia has resulted not in the redistribution of riches but to a large extent in their destruction.[13]

---

[12] Joseph A. Schumpeter, *Capitalism, Socialism, and Democracy,* New York, Harper, 1947, pp. 125-126. For a similar but slightly more cautious statement of this same position by an eminent British economist see Thomas Wilson, *Modern Capitalism and Economic Progress,* London, Macmillan, 1950, Chaps. I, II.

[13] Boulding, *op. cit.,* p. 665. The concluding statement is completely at variance with current studies of Soviet production—e. g., Alexander Baykov, *The Development of the Soviet Economic System,* Cambridge, Harvard University Press, 1947. See, especially the summary statement on Soviet production on pp. 302-303.

The extreme importance attached to capitalism by the classicist is related to his theory of economic progress. Since it is in capitalism that the extremes of income distribution exist sufficient to promote individual savings, and since savings are necessary to capital accumulation, only under capitalism is continued progress guaranteed.

Not until the past two decades has the classicist had any serious qualms about the continuation of progress under a beneficent capitalism. Nevertheless, he did have some fears from time to time over the continuation of the process of accumulation. The advent of the stationary state has been a question of serious concern to classicists, and at times it has been a wolfish specter at the door of capitalist theory. Thus classical theory has suffered periods of pessimism when the stationary state seemed imminent and periods of optimism when it appeared remote.

At its inception in the economics of Adam Smith, classical theory was optimistic. Adam Smith was an eighteenth-century moral philosopher who turned his attention to economic matters. As such, his thought was pervaded by the optimism of the eighteenth century. This optimism was based on the belief in the continued moral uplift and ultimate perfectability of mankind. Smith's economic system in its logic did not necessarily lead to optimism, but the general outlook of the author was one of optimism. As Veblen has stated, "there are many passages that testify to his abiding convictions that there is a wholesome trend in the natural course of things . . ."[14]

In Smith's theory the process of accumulation was of significance for economic progress. It was by accumulation that capital was increased, and by increasing capital a greater division of labor would be made possible.[15] The division of labor was important; for by a greater division of labor the "skill, dexterity, and judgment" of the labor force, the more important of two major factors accounting for the wealth of nations, was enhanced.[16] For the person who uses his stock to employ productive labor is endowed with a natural desire to increase the output of that labor. This leads to the development of

---

[14] Veblen, *The Place of Science*, p. 114.

[15] Adam Smith, *The Wealth of Nations*, p. 260.

[16] *Ibid.*, p. lvii.

new labor-saving machines and contrivances. Not only does the labor of a country turn out a greater amount of wealth with the accumulation of stock for its employment, but this very accumulation has a tendency to enhance the output of labor.[17]

That accumulation meant to Adam Smith pecuniary, not machine and tool, accumulation is evident from the fact that he held parsimony to be the source of accumulation. Capitals are "diminished by prodigality and misconduct" and are enhanced by parsimonious behavior.[18] Since capital accumulation is dependent upon parsimony, Smith thought it fortunate for the progress of mankind that nature had designed a reasonable man who is by natural bent a parsimonious creature. There are prodigals who by improvident living dissipate the capital that has been accumulated, but the high living of these wastrels is not sufficient to offset the product of the more parsimonious.[19] Although private prodigality and misconduct cannot stay the path of progress by destroying the fruits of past accumulation, nations are sometimes impoverished by "public prodigality and misconduct."[20] But even the most lavish spending by improvident governments in most instances is not sufficient to overcome the results of the desire of every man to improve his position by saving. In fact, this principle prompting us to save "comes with us from the womb, and never leaves till we go into the grave."[21] That Smith has pecuniary accumulation in mind is clear from his use of prodigality. Prodigals spend family fortunes and reduce the pecuniary worth of the family. They play fast and loose with money funds, not with tools and machines.

For present purposes Adam Smith may be said to have established a general pattern for the economic theorist to follow. From the time of Smith to the present no classicist has doubted that capital is accumulated through saving.

There have been those like Malthus and Keynes who have worried about flaws in this accumulation process, and there have been others like J. S. Mill and J. B. Clark who have con-

---

17 *Ibid.*, p. 260.
18 *Ibid.*, p. 321.
19 *Ibid.*, p. 324.
20 *Ibid.*, p. 325.
21 *Ibid.*, p. 324.

cerned themselves about the advent of the stationary state, but none, Keynes excepted, has held the saving process to be any more than the accumulation process by which capital is created.

Ricardo was one whose theory, when followed to its logical conclusions, was pessimistic. Yet it cannot be denied that Ricardo accepted the accumulation process as the source of capital, meaning tools and machines. The pessimism of Ricardian theory was injected by Malthus. Where Smith had seen a beneficent natural order, Malthus saw a natural order characterized by perpetual poverty. *The Wealth of Nations* was written in 1776 before the effects of a new industrialism had been felt. The miseries of rural poverty had not yet been raked up, concentrated, and dumped into the new factory towns for all to see. But by the turn of the century the new industrial order was apparent on all fronts and the new factory towns were not a pretty sight to behold. In addition, the population of Britain had been increasing and in the last decade of the eighteenth century the island for the first time had to resort to importation of grains to feed its rising population.

Malthus marks the end of the optimism of the eighteenth century. From his time on, poverty has been viewed as a function of natural law, the natural law of population. Where the classical optimism had viewed poverty as a temporary thing that would be eliminated by the natural progress of opulence, poverty was now viewed as a permanent and inevitable condition of the general run of the population. The glory of the Malthusian law of population was that it seemingly rested on irrefutable evidence apparent to the common sense of all. In addition it rested on a so-called fundamental law of the physical universe, diminishing returns. The new "science" of population was eagerly seized upon by those who were only too anxious to wipe out any compunctions over poverty by concluding its inevitability, and by those who had been frightened by the "excesses" of the French Revolution.[22] This natural law "proved" that existent social institutions were not responsible for poverty.

Malthus would not be of great concern to the present inquiry if it were not for the fact that when his population doctrine

[22] J. B. Bury, *The Idea of Progress,* London, Macmillan, 1928, pp. 227-228.

was combined with the economics of Adam Smith by Ricardo, the result was to make of classical theory a "dismal science." Although Ricardo, like all classicists before and after, held that the secret of progress was in the accumulation process, the result of his theory was to cast some doubt on the continuation of that process. In other words, the logical result of Ricardian theory was that specter of classical political economy, the stationary state. This consequence was the result of Ricardo's accepting the population doctrine of Malthus at face value.

In the Ricardian system a falling rate of profit was inevitable, because Ricardo accepted Malthus unquestioningly. Although Ricardo held that his main concern was with the determinants of income distribution within that system of organization bounded by landlord, capitalist, and laborer,[23] a dynamic is implicit in the Ricardian system.[24] This dynamic is teleological, for it is working toward the stationary state. The dynamic element is Malthus' theory of population. For in the Ricardian system it is the pressure of population on the means of subsistence that causes a resort to poorer and poorer grades of the one fixed factor of production, land. As a result, diminishing returns are realized per unit of labor applied more intensively or on the margin of cultivation.

To Ricardo, progress took place as the advance of the productive process made possible an increase of wealth. An increase of wealth depended upon an increase of commodities. Thus, in the progress of society, wealth might be increased by "the invention of machinery, by improvements in skill, by a better division of labor, or by the discovery of new markets where more advantageous exchanges may be made."[25] This is a key point in Ricardian theory, for in the progress of society there was one factor, land, which was limited in amount. As the population was augmented in keeping with the enhanced wealth of the community, it would be necessary to resort to poorer and poorer grades of land and to more intensive cultivation, which would mean an increase in the value of wage goods. Thus, wages would rise, profits would fall, accumulation would fail,

---

23 Ricardo, *The Principles of Political Economy*, p. 1.
24 Halévy, *The Growth of Philosophic Radicalism*, p. 319.
25 Ricardo, *op. cit.*, p. 182.

and a stagnation of wealth accumulation and population would usher in a static society.

Ricardo, like Smith, related capital accumulation to progress. With a fall in profits the incentive to accumulate would be weakened, accumulation would cease, and progress through capital expansion would be jeopardized.

> Without a motive there could be no accumulation and consequently such a state of prices never could take place. The farmer and manufacturer can no more live without profit than the labourer without wages. Their motive for accumulation will diminish with every diminution of profit, and will cease altogether when their profits are so low as not to afford them an adequate compensation for their trouble, and the risk which they must necessarily encounter in employing their capital productively.[26]

Ricardo is also quite clear on the means by which accumulation takes place. As with all classicists, capital accumulation is the result of saving.

> There are two ways in which capital may be accumulated, it may be saved either in consequence of increased revenue or of diminished consumption.[27]

In the long-run passage of time and with the increase of population, a unit of labor brings a diminished return, the money wages of all labor are raised, profits fall, saving is diminished, accumulation ceases, and progress comes to a halt. In the Ricardian system the stationary state is imminent.

John Stuart Mill has frequently been looked upon as a carbon copy of Ricardo in expanded form, but this is not altogether the case. Mill lived during that period in which the rise of modern industrialism was unmistakable. In theory Mill was a Ricardian pessimist, but when he looked out upon the world about him he was an optimist. In this sense Mill is a forerunner of the later neoclassical optimism.

Mill held that "the requisites of production are labour and appropriate natural objects." Labor tends to increase in accordance with the Malthusian geometric progression, so that it cannot fail to expand with the needs of the economy. But labor is aided and abetted in its production of wealth by capital,

---

[26] *Ibid.*, p. 73.
[27] *Ibid.*, p. 79.

meaning, of course, tools and implements. Capital is accumulated by discretion in consumption expenditures, or in the words which Mill borrowed from Senior, by abstinence. Abstinence, of course, is synonymous with saving. So, to sum up, capital is the product of saving, meaning the saving of money funds. The only limitation on saving is the willingness of income receivers to stint.

But at this point in his theory, Mill, like Ricardo, reverts to Malthusian pessimism. Land is a limited quantity and, although some economists have overlooked this matter, it is one of the most significant facts of political economy.[28] Population constantly presses against the ability of this limited amount of land to maintain subsistence. Thus progress is limited by land. But Mill, with the new optimism of the mid-nineteenth century, opens a large loophole in the Malthusian argument.

> There is another agency in habitual antagonism to the law of diminishing return from land; . . . it is no other than the progress of civilization. I use this general and somewhat vague expression, because the things to be included are so various, that hardly any term of a more restricted signification would comprehend them all.[29]

Mill takes cognizance of technological advance in the arts of production. The agencies working at cross purposes to the law of diminishing returns make possible an increase in the produce of agriculture without a more than proportionate increase in the necessary amount of labor. "Of these, the most obvious is the progress of agricultural knowledge, skill, and invention."[30] Other factors that contribute to the alleviation of the effects of the pressure of the population on the means of raising foodstuffs are improved means of communication and "many purely mechancial improvements, which have apparently at least, no peculiar connexion with agriculture, nevertheless enable a given amount of food to be obtained with a smaller expenditure of labour."[31] In fact the progress of agriculture may be such as to require a constantly increasing amount of labor per unit of output, yet the standard of living may rise as a consequence of the fact that labor is becoming

28 Mill, *Principles of Political Economy,* p. 176.
29 *Ibid.,* p. 183.
30 *Ibid.*
31 *Ibid.,* p. 184.

so much more proficient in other productive pursuits that more than enough laborers could be released for this increased need for labor in agriculture.[32]

Here, of course, is a large loophole in the Malthusian argument. Mill was living and writing in an age when the world was becoming conscious of the effects of what, before his death, would be called "The Industrial Revolution" by Arnold Toynbee in a historically significant series of lectures. Here is the beginning of a new optimism which arose as a consequence of the rapid and apparent strides made by industrialism in the nineteenth century, a change that was to bring back into the stream of traditionally accepted economic thought the optimism of the eighteenth century. There was one difference, however. The earlier optimism was based on a faith in the perfectability of man; the later was an optimism based on the perfectability of a prolific industrial machine. But Mill, being habituated to Malthusian-Ricardian pessimism, made no more of the point.

Although Mill did not follow his observation through to the logical breakdown of Malthusianism in economic theory, it can be said that his optimism tied Mill to the neoclassical optimism. In fact it was specifically on this ground of technological advance that the neoclassicists rejected Malthusianism and brought back into political economy the optimistic harmony of Adam Smith. Nevertheless, Mill, like all classicists, still clung to the idea that accumulation of money funds was the way of progress. Technology was all right for upsetting Malthusianism, but the explanation of progress needed something more than "mere" technology. That this is the case is illustrated by the concluding paragraph in Mill's chapter on "The Stationary State."[33]

In theory Mill, like Ricardo, held that the teleological end of capitalism is the stationary state. But what does he mean by the stationary state? The following passage shows that, like all classicists, he means a state of no net-saving.

> It is scarcely necessary to remark that a stationary condition of capital and population implies no stationary state of human improvement. . . . Even the industrial arts might be as earnestly and as successfully cultivated, with this sole difference, that instead of

---

32 *Ibid.*, p. 186.
33 *Ibid.*, p. 751.

serving no purpose but the increase of wealth, industrial improvements would produce their legitimate effect, that of abridging labour.[34]

Nowhere in classical political economy, with the possible exception of Keynes' *General Theory*,[35] is there a passage which more clearly illustrates the classical concept of progress. All classicists, like Mill, differentiate between money and wealth, holding the latter to be material wealth. The stationary state is conceived as one in which progress has ceased. But progress, supposedly, has meant a growth of wealth. This has been the result of technological advance. Yet in the above passage technological advance would continue in the stationary state. Then why not wealth? Simply because, when put in this fashion, wealth to Mill and all of the classicists does mean pecuniary wealth and not material wealth. Progress is nothing but pecuniary accumulation. Technological advance is truly something else.

Nevertheless, recognition of technological advance rang the death knell of Malthusianism and returned to classicism the optimism of Adam Smith. There were outside influences working to turn theory in this direction. Although the industrial revolution had gone into high gear during the eighteenth century, the full effect and significance of the new industrialism was not then realized by classical political economy. However, by the last quarter of the nineteenth century its effects were so momentous that the facts could no longer be denied. A new optimism pervaded men's thinking, for it was felt that the industrial progress so typical of that era would bring about a continued and rapid economic progress.

The advances in the steel-making process are typical of the advances in many industrial areas. In the seventies the converter process of making iron into steel had been perfected simultaneously and independently by Kelley in the United States and Bessemer in England, taking its name from the latter. This new process made it feasible to turn out steel rails in sufficient quantity to give a new impetus to railroad building. Heavier and longer trains could now be operated, making the

34 *Ibid.*

35 Keynes, *The General Theory*, pp. 220-221.

railroad the chief means of transportation. In the eighties the open-hearth process for making steel was developed which made possible higher grades of steel than had been possible with the Bessemer process. These developments in steel manifested themselves throughout the industrial economy, making possible a new abundance. But steel was only one of the more outstanding achievements in the momentous industrial progress that typified the whole latter half of the nineteenth century. Constant improvements in manufacturing methods and processes were characteristic of the period.[36]

These technological improvements were working toward the general rise of the standard of living. It seemed that a new abundance was about to overtake mankind and that life would become a thing of beauty for all. Under the influence of these strides in technological progress Malthusianism could not long endure. Of course, Malthus did not depreciate technological progress, but he did hold that insofar as products depending upon the soil for their cultivation were concerned, technological progress was a temporary palliative that could not possibly stay the effects of population growth. In theory Mill was a Malthusian, although, as has been shown, he weakened his Malthusian position. But by the time of neoclassicism, technological advance had begun to show noticeable effects in agriculture as well as industry. In addition, the American plains had by this time come into production. With the improvements in transportation this bread basket was available to the world.

The total export of wheat in 1860 was 17,000,000 bushels; it rose three years later to 58,000,000; at the end of the century it had gone well over the 200,000,000 mark. While advance agents for the cotton spinners of England and ironmongers of Germany, in the piping days that followed the Franco-German War, marched with measured tread into the backward and waste places of Asia, Africa, and South America and invaded islands of distant seas, the farmers of the United States poured their swelling avalanche of wheat, corn, and pork into the markets of Europe to supply food for the laborers of Manchester, Birmingham, and Essen. With true insight, a distinguished Austrian economist declared that the flow of American agricultural produce to the Old World in the latter part of the nineteenth century made a revolution in its economy comparable

36 Lewis Mumford, *Technics and Civilization,* New York, Harcourt Brace, 1934, pp. 205-210, Chap. V.

to that produced by the flow of gold and silver in the age that succeeded the discoveries of Columbus.[37]

The grim outlook of the first two decades of the nineteenth century could not be sustained in the last two decades of the century. Malthusianism had to give way before industrialism. But Malthusianism had been one of the chief props of Ricardian political economy. As doubt developed on the validity of the population doctrine, the way was open for a more optimistic view of things.

In neoclassicism the harmonious optimism of Adam Smith was reestablished. Since Malthusianism was no longer tenable, it was held that there was no tendency for population to press against the means of subsistence. Land was no longer a limiting factor. True, profits might fall, but this was because of a bad proportion among the factors of production. The returns to each of the factors were now explained by means of marginal productivity, and a reduction in the return to one would simply call for readjustments in the proportions of each. In the hands of Alfred Marshall and J. B. Clark, economics became similar to the study of the compensatory movements of three balls in a goldfish bowl. There was no reason for fear, however, because progress was unlimited. Capital accumulation could go on forever without any reason for abatement. There were disturbing elements, but these did not threaten progress. They were merely cause for readjustment in economic statics. These disturbing elements were the dynamics of J. B. Clark.

It was not until J. M. Keynes' *General Theory* that this rosy view of things was questioned by a reputable economist. Malthus and Hobson had both challenged the idea that accumulation could never be excessive. Nevertheless, it is to be noted that neither one of these two heretical economists challenged the idea that capital accumulation was the product of saving, and in this sense both Malthus and Hobson were true to the central core of classical economics. But John Maynard Keynes did challenge the classical concept in his *General Theory* and so injected a new pessimism into the classical stream.

---

[37] Charles A. and Mary R. Beard, *The Rise of American Civilization,* New York, Macmillan, 1930, Vol. 2, pp. 257-258.

Say's law of markets was essential to the classical theory of progress. Although Ricardo is most frequently cited as one of the first to resort to the argument attributed to Say, Adam Smith could be quoted to the same effect, and he antedates both Say and Ricardo.

What is annually saved is as regularly consumed as what is annually spent, and nearly in the same time too; but it is consumed by a different set of people. That portion of his revenue which a rich man annually spends, is in most cases consumed by idle guests, and menial servants, who leave nothing behind them in return for their consumption. That portion which he annually saves, as for the sake of the profit it is immediately employed as a capital, is consumed in the same manner, and nearly in the same time too, but by a different set of people, by labourers, manufacturers, and artificers, who re-produce with a profit the value of their annual consumption.[38]

The major attack by Keynes on the classical doctrine fell on that part known as Say's law of markets. This was held by Keynes to be one of the major assumptions on which the classical theory of employment rested.[39] But this assumption is illusory and this whole way of thinking a deception.

Those who think in this way are deceived, nevertheless, by an optical illusion, which makes two essentially different activities appear to be the same. They are fallaciously supposing that there is a nexus which unites decisions to abstain from present consumption with decisions to provide for future consumption; whereas the notions which determine the latter are not linked in any simple way with the motives which determine the former.[40]

Since Say's law is invalid, it follows that classical optimism is based on error. Pecuniary accumulation may proceed, but this pecuniary accumulation is not necessarily identical with capital accumulation. Keynes makes this quite clear in his analysis of liquidity. According to classical doctrine no one would choose to hold money for any period of time over and above that necessary to living in a pecuniary civilization. In other words, a certain amount of money might be held in order to facilitate purchase and sale, and some money might be held for contingencies, but no one would hoard money. Keynes

38 Adam Smith, *op. cit.*, p. 321.
39 J. M. Keynes, *op. cit.*, pp. 21-22.
40 *Ibid.*, p. 21.

shows, however, that individuals do hoard money, that they have a penchant for liquidity and desire to hold varying amounts of money according to the economic situation. There are, in brief, three reasons why people desire to hold money: (1) the transactions motive, (2) the precautionary motive, (3) the speculative motive.[41] Of these motives the first two are rather stable at any one level of economic activity but the last is extremely variable and depends on anticipations of variations in the rate of interest.[42] That is, when a rise in the rate of interest is anticipated over and above that "assumed by the market," the inducement of those affected by the speculative motive is to hold money. When a fall in the rate of interest below that assumed by the market is anticipated, the inducement is to hold debt.[43] But the significant fact is that people do use money as a store of value, a fact which had been neglected by the traditional economics.

Thus, investment and saving are two separate and distinct acts. Attempts to save more, if not offset by additional investment, will result in a reduction in income and employment and so a reduction in the amount saved. There is no longer any reason to assume that increased savings mean increased progress. Increased attempts to save may mean a decrease in income, employment, and savings, the reverse of economic progress.

In fact Keynes envisages increased difficulties in the future in maintaining a level of investment sufficient to equate income with full employment. This is a consequence of the tendency of the marginal efficiency of capital to fall in the long run, reducing the stimulus to new investment. On these grounds he advocates governmental policy to maintain full employment. In other words, there is no assurance in classical theory as left by Keynes that we shall not attain the stationary state in which there is no net capital accumulation.

On such assumption I should guess that a properly run community equipped with modern technical resources, of which the population is not increasing rapidly, ought to be able to bring down the marginal efficiency of capital in equilibrium approximately to zero

41 *Ibid.*, pp. 170, 195-196.

42 *Ibid.*, pp. 196-197.

43 *Ibid.*, p. 170.

within a single generation; so that we should attain the conditions of a quasi-stationary community where change and progress would result only from changes in technique, taste, population and institutions, with the products of capital selling at a price proportional to the labour, etc., embodied in them on just the same principles as govern the prices of consumption-goods into which capital charges enter in an insignificant degree.[44]

This is a remarkable passage from one standpoint. It identifies Keynes with the classical school in so far as progress is concerned. Although Keynes is looked upon as a revolutionist in economic theory, his revolution, like all revolutions, is by no means a complete break with the past. As was pointed out above,[45] Mill made almost the same statement in a passage on the stationary state. Keynes, of course, differs from Mill and all other classicists in that he does not identify accumulation and progress. Nevertheless, the above quotation makes it clear that Keynes does not identify progress with "mere technological" advance. For in the stationary state "change and progress would result only from changes in technique, taste, population, and institutions." Thus, in the non-stationary state progress must result from something else. What is this if it is not saving? It is investment. But since investment is clearly a pecuniary phenomenon, and since Keynes has separated "changes in technique" from investment, then progress is identical with investment, which in turn is a process of pecuniary capitalization. It can mean nothing else. Thus, Keynes, like all classicists, sees progress as a pecuniary phenomenon.

It might be well to ask at this point why all classicists have identified progress with some aspect of pecuniary manipulation? Why has progress been associated with the enhancement of pecuniary values? And why has technological change been taken for granted? For one thing, the classicist has focused his attention on the individual—society being to him nothing but a collection of individuals. What is important from this standpoint has been the capitalist. It has been the "man of vision," the "entrepreneur," the "innovator," the "man of action," in contrast to the "thinker," the "tinkerer," the "inventor," to whom has been attributed great mystic potency analo-

---

[44] *Ibid.*, pp. 220-221.

[45] See above, pp. 111-112.

gous to that attributed to the primitive medicine man. Matter-of-fact workmanship by an organized group is not sufficient. There must be someone in a coercive role to whom is attributed an ability which is not describable in matter-of-fact terms. The individual must possess "vision," "foresight," "initiative," and "enterprise," qualities that are not possessed by all men but are manifest only in "business leaders." Evidence of possession of such qualities is attested by the position of the individual. Since he is in such a position, he must possess these qualities, for otherwise he would not be in the position.

In present-day society the businessman or capitalist is in a role that in the past has been granted to or usurped by warriors, royalty, and priests. All of these individuals are workers of great feats that no ordinary man could perform. They work wonders that give to their activities a dramatic flair. Attention has always been centered on these actors within the ceremonial aspect of culture. Those who perform more workmanlike tasks that lend themselves to a matter-of-fact recounting are not dramatic and are not worthy of attention.

What does the businessman do? He works magic with money funds. He makes two shares of stock exist where but one existed before. He enhances pecuniary values. But what is of more import is the fact that in doing this he supposedly "creates" hotels, steamships, and railroads where none existed before. Thus, progress has been associated with his activities. A mystic potency has been ascribed to money and to monetary manipulation which fits into the general Newtonianism of the classicist. He has been concerned with those principles determining the "nature and causes of the wealth of nations" from the time of Adam Smith. What are the maxims governing the growth of the wealth of nations? Despite Smith's criticisms of the mercantilists, the classicist has been no less concerned with the increase of money values than the mercantilist. As has been demonstrated, implicit in the whole classical literature has been a conception of progress as pecuniary growth. The whole set of classical principles is tied together by the role of these principles in assuring progress. In fact some, such as Smith and the neoclassicists, have viewed the economic universe as a naturally harmonious one in which progress would continue uninhibited. Others, such as Ricardo and Keynes, have seen reasons for alarm. Nevertheless, all have held progress to be a process of pecuniary enhancement within a fixed social scheme.

Their ideas on progress are Newtonian in character and are related to their concepts of psychology and of the social system. Individuals enhance pecuniary values because a provident nature has endowed them with a propensity "to truck, barter, and exchange one thing for another." They do this in an eternal social arrangement. Human nature is stable and the social system is stable. The only thing subject to change is pecuniary values. Technological change, making possible a better and less precarious living, is taken for granted. The acquisition of pecuniary wealth and its enhancement by all individuals is looked upon as progress on the national level.

Unlike the classicist, the institutionalist does not simply take technological change for granted. Progress is identified with the advance of science and technology. This aspect of institutional economics is manifest in the amount of interest the institutionalist shows in the progressive development of technology. In the usual classical treatise, a mention of technology is incidental to the major task in hand, the exposition of pecuniary principles. In the institutional treatise, technology and its impact on social organization is frequently the central theme of the book.[46] To the institutionalist, the industrial revolution is of prime importance, for it has brought profound changes in the economic life process.[47]

To the institutionalist, taking culture as his field of inquiry, it is apparent that the dynamic aspect of culture is technology. As was pointed out above, culture has a static and a dynamic aspect. That which is static is the institutional side of culture; that which is dynamic is its technological aspect.

But what makes technology dynamic? Why is it subject to change? This is the aspect of culture that is subject to growth through trait combination or invention and it is this process of growth that makes technology dynamic. All of this has been stated in the previous chapter, but it is necessary briefly to re-

---

46 See for instance Walton Hamilton, *Price and Price Policies,* New York, McGraw-Hill, 1938.

47 C. E. Ayres, *The Problem of Economic Order,* New York, Farrar and Rinehart, 1938, pp. 3-19.

state it, for the institutionalist's view of progress is closely associated with his concept of cultural growth. It is likewise this aspect of institutionalism that raises the most serious objections from those among whom the idea "progress" is in ill repute. To be sure, progress has frequently been viewed as a teleological cultural unfolding culminating in the existing or projected ideal culture of the viewer. This aspect of human thought has been called "ethnocentric." Critics have been quick to point out that all groups have held that their culture is superior to all others. Thus all such judgments seem to be relative to the communities which hold them. Who is to judge the superiority of the Christian religion over that of the Zuni? But this analysis ends in the dilemma in which the *mores* become the final arbiter of the *mores.* This was essentially the position in which Sumner left the problem in his *Folkways.* And it is the position today of nearly all of those who, however rightfully, are wary of ethnocentrism.

But there is more to be said on the question than at first meets the eye. Those who have taken the above position have done notable service in disposing of ethnocentrism. On the other hand, their failure to go any further with the argument comes from their lumping together all aspects of culture and calling them institutions. It is this kind of thinking about culture that leads institutional economists, such as Russell Dixon, to call technology an institution. Likewise it leads to treating progress as merely a figment of the imagination, a matter of one's point of view. The following quotation is typical of this idea.

Progress is the term ordinarily used to characterize changes which are believed to improve a situation. Obviously, all progress constitutes change but all change is not progress. *Progress is an interpretation of change* and not an inherent characteristic. Social change can only be termed progress when it results in more nearly attaining some goal or objective. The invention and acceptance by the group of a lamp more nearly approximating sunlight represents progress only to those who regard sunlight as the best type of illumination. To those who believe that the ultra-violet rays of sunlight are detrimental to health, the invention and use of a lamp producing them would be a change not toward but away from their goal of good health. The same change would therefore be interpreted as progress by persons with one goal or objective and retrogression by those with a different one.[48]

This attitude toward progress has been prompted by the extreme ethnocentrism of those who have attributed all progress to a particular race or nationality. Dixon is perfectly correct when he states that "all change is not progress." What he fails to do, like all others who take this position, is to differentiate between that aspect of culture which is ceremonial in nature and that which is technological. Veblen made this differentiation, and that is why he and those who have taken the same path have a theory of progress.

Such a theory must answer the following questions. (1) Is all culture identical? (2) Is there some aspect of culture that is subject to cumulative development in which it is possible to demonstrate progress? The institutionalist, as was indicated in the last chapter, answers the first question negatively. Culture has ceremonial and technological aspects. It is with the answer to the second that this chapter is mainly concerned.

As was shown previously, culture is subject to a process of cumulative change. But this is not true of all culture. It is true of those aspects of culture which the institutionalist calls technological. Veblen made this process of cumulative development synonymous with the development of science and technology—that is, "matter-of-fact knowledge." Cultures can be distinguished and the cultural development of mankind can be demonstrated through the development of this "matter-of-fact" or technological aspect of culture. It is the larger part played by this aspect of culture in "modern Christendom" that distinguishes it from all other cultures past and present.

> Modern Civilisation is peculiarly matter-of-fact. It contains many elements that are not of this character, but these other elements do not belong exclusively or characteristically to it. The modern civilised peoples are in a peculiar degree capable of an impersonal, dispassionate insight into the material facts with which mankind has to deal.[49]

---

48 R. A. Dixon and E. Kingman Eberhart, *Economics and Cultural Change*, pp. 16-17.

49 Veblen, *The Place of Science*, p. 1.

The constant theme throughout all the work of Veblen was the clash between the uninhibited development of matter of fact and the institutions. In some cases the argument took the form of the clash between matter-of-fact knowledge and myth;[50] in other places the clash is between industry and business;[51] in still others it is between workmanship and predation.[52] But always the discussion centers on the growth of technology and its inhibition by "imbecile institutions."

In each case it is clear that Veblen identified progress with the growth of technology, with the free development of workmanship, and with the growth of matter of fact. This point appears clearly in the following passage:

> In the cases where it has happened that those instincts which make directly for the material welfare of the community, such as the parental bent and the sense of workmanship, have been present in such potent force, or where the institutional elements at variance with the continued life-interests of the community or the civilization in question have been in a sufficiently infirm state, there the bonds of custom, prescription, principles, precedent, have been broken—or loosened or shifted so as to let the current of life and cultural growth go on, with or without substantial retardation. But history records more frequent and more spectacular instances of the triumph of imbecile institutions over life and culture than of peoples who have by force of instinctive insight saved themselves alive out of a desperately precarious institutional situation, such, for instance as now faces the peoples of Christendom.[53]

As is clear from the above, Veblen held that progress or cultural growth will take place when the growth of matter-of-fact knowledge is uninhibited by custom or "imbecile institutions." By no means does Veblen hold progress to be inevitable, a cultural imperative following from the existence of workmanship. Workmanship may be "contaminated" and turned to account in "predation." This is clearly the case of the cultures of Asia Minor, the Aegean region, Egypt, and Rome. Here institutions, or custom in the form of a coercive regime organized for predatory pursuits, worked at cross purposes to workmanship with

---

[50] *Ibid.*, pp. 5-20, 40-46.

[51] Veblen, *The Theory of Business Enterprise, The Engineers and the Price System, Absentee Ownership.*

[52] Veblen, *The Theory of the Leisure Class, The Instinct of Workmanship, The Nature of Peace.*

[53] Veblen, *The Instinct of Workmanship,* p. 25.

the result that "these great civilizations dominated by pastoral antecedents have no grave significance for the modern culture, except as drawbacks, and none at all for modern technology or for that matter-of-fact knowledge on which modern technology runs."[54]

Likewise, Veblen is by no means certain that present-day institutions will not triumph over technology. This he makes clear in the closing pages of *The Theory of Business Enterprise.* The machine technology has been a disintegrative force exerted on ancient customs and prescriptive. In other words, workmanship has been in the ascendency and predation has been falling by the wayside. Nevertheless, there is no assurance that such a state of things will continue to prevail. Predation may triumph in the end.[55]

Progress is found by Veblen in what Professor Ayres calls the technological continuum.[56] That aspect of culture which the institutionalist has termed technology is continuous and subject to cumulative development. It is at this point that the thought of institutionalism and that of the "instrumental" school of philosophy converge. What is continuous in technology to the institutionalist is the process of valuation. Although he did not state the case in the same terms, what Veblen called the growth of matter of fact is identical with what Dewey calls the continuum of ends-means.[57] This has been noted by Professor Ayres who has called attention to the similarity between Dewey and Veblen on this ground. To Dewey, life is a continuous process of adjustment, of devising means to achieve ends-in-view, themselves means to further ends-in-view, etc. This is what Ayres calls the life process, and this is what the institutionalist calls technological progress. For it is in the technological aspect of culture that this continuous growth and adjustment are found.

Of course the question of the ultimate ends of life is always raised. The cultural relativist claims that the institutionalist has found an ultimate end in technology. Since values are held by

---

54 *Ibid.*, p. 170.

55 Veblen, *The Theory of Business Enterprise*, pp. 398-399.

56 Ayres, *The Theory of Economic Progress*, pp. 220 ff.

57 John Dewey, "The Theory of Valuation," *International Encyclopedia of Unified Science*, Chicago, University of Chicago Press, 1947, pp. 40 ff.

the relativist to be subjective, the institutionalist by identifying progress with technological development is merely demonstrating his particular set of values. This is the position taken by the classicist who is critical of the institutionalist. In fact the classicist, by locating the measure of value in the price system seeks to avoid the issue of valuation. Since price is simply an objective measure of the subjective valuations of all of the individual members of society, the classicist claims to avoid the issue of value by the objective study of the market. People like what they like and that is all there is to be said. There is no disputing tastes!

To this the institutionalist replies that this is not the issue.[58] For one thing, the idea of ultimate ends is a product of that dualism in human thought that can be traced back to primitive times and is especially clear in the thought of the Greeks, particularly Plato. Likewise, ultimate ends have been manifest in institutions which are encrustations of ancient prescriptive and holy writ, not subject to further and continuous verification. Ultimate ends are the product of ancient myth. But all ancient prescriptive purports to be based on fact and purports to be in the interest of the material welfare of the group.[59] For instance, the old adage that a woman's place is in the home was more than a mos. At one time woman's place in the home was actually related to material well-being. It was an effective part of the whole stream of life activities. Nevertheless, as a mos this kind of tradition is not subject to empirical verification, and it is this aspect of human culture in which "ultimate ends" are embodied in the mores and authenticated by myth that is called institutional.

To the institutionalist the whole idea of "ultimate ends" is a product of the dualism of ancient thought which was manifested in a dualism in life itself. In institutionalist economic theory, progress is the cumulative development of technology. It is not progress in the direction of some transcendental end, nor is it the worship of tools for tools' sake. No one denies this cumulative growth. What some object to is the fact that progress

---

58 For remarkably similar positions from another quarter see the recent volume by Barbara Wooton, *Testament for Social Science*, New York, Norton, 1950, Chap. VI. See also C. H. Waddington, *The Scientific Attitude*, Great Britain, Penguin Books, 1948, Chap. II, "Science Is Not Neutral."

59 Ayres, *op. cit.*, pp. 217 ff.

is identified with the continuity of technology. Progress has always been considered something more, an unfolding toward some Ultimate. It is this last piece of ancient institutional furniture that the institutionalists have abandoned. It is not a case of replacing some ultimate or transcendental end by a new one. What the institutionalist has abandoned is the idea of an ultimate end, a concept that found its authentication in institutionalized thought patterns. The attitude of the institutionalists on this issue is similar to what Veblen said about the disappearance of institutions: "A man who loses a wart off the end of his nose does not apply to the *Ersatz* bureau for a convenient substitute."[60]

Thus, institutionalism is in a sense optimistic. There is no technological reason why mankind cannot solve the economic problems that beset him. He may not do so, but then again there is no reason to prove that he will not do so. As Professor Ayres has stated the case, "No one any longer doubts the physical and technological possibility of a worldwide economy of abundance."[61] The same train of thought was noted by Professor Daugert in the concluding paragraph of his study of the philosophy of Veblen.

> Important as the disciplinary effect of the machine process may be, what is even more important is Veblen's view that the present state of the industrial arts is easily and fully capable of providing for human needs. In fact, he asserts, modern industry is "inordinately productive." There is no sound technological reason why humanity must do without essential needs, why it must suffer periodic crises and depressions. The resources for solving the economic problems of human needs, human wants, and human desires *exist*. It remains for us to plan to use these resources intelligently, to solve these problems scientifically, equitably, and economically.[62]

In the light of the rise of modern industrialism, the position of the classicist is odd indeed. No one can deny that the general lot of mankind has been raised with the development of machine industry. This development has been increasingly accelerated throughout the period of dominance of classical political economy, i.e., from the time of Adam Smith to the present. In

---

60 Veblen, *The Nature of Peace*, p. 216.
61 Ayres, *op. cit.*, p. 232.
62 Daugert, *Philosophy of Veblen*, p. 103.

other words, what is called the "Industrial Revolution" has been paralleled by the rise and dominance of classical political economy. Throughout this time the effect of the industrial revolution has been an improved standard of living, evidenced by the increase in population and longevity. Yet during this very time of increasing material welfare, classical political economy has been at times optimistic, but has been just as frequently pessimistic as to the future lot of mankind.

This aspect of classical political economy is in contrast with that of institutionalism, which has been consistently optimistic. Wherein lies the difference? The classicist has focused his major attention on the price system and on quantitative change, mechanically measured by price. In true Newtonian style, he has sought the principles that govern the mechanical changes of this natural economic system. He has taken technology and the continuity of tool development for granted and has sought the "real" explanation of the nature and causes of the wealth of nations in the price system. But the institutionalist claims the price system has repeatedly disrupted the continuity of the technological process. The price system is a ceremonial system which is repeatedly menaced by the increasing productivity of modern technology. Profit, the end-all of the price system, is threatened by the immense productivity of a non-scarcity technological system. Classical theory, attributing great significance to the price system, becomes pessimistic when that system seems threatened, optimistic when that system seems to be going well. No other explanation is possible for the rapid swing of classical economists to Keynes in the late nineteen-thirties, and the present haste of many economists to deny the relevancy of Keynesianism. Among present-day classicists it is becoming popular to allude to Keynesian economics as a special case—a depression situation—even though Keynes held his theory to be a general theory and therefore not applicable to depression analysis only. These fluctuations in outlook on the part of the classicists, despite obvious improvement in material welfare, result from the classicist's concentration of attention on "rationalizing" the price system.

Institutionalism, on the other hand, has been relatively optimistic. This might be attributed to the fact that institutionalism has given to technological development a major place in economic theory during a period of startling technological advance. But there is more to be said on the matter. Institutionalism is Darwinian, not Newtonian. It is evolutionary, not mechanical. It is concerned with cumulative change, not with a series of discrete movements. Progress is seen as the process of cumulative technological development. A continuity can be seen in the progressive development of technology. The digging stick gives way to the spade, the spade to the plow, the wood plow to the iron plow, the iron plow to the steel plow, the horse-pulled steel plow to the tractor-pulled gang plow. Each one of these changes can be shown to be dependent on the previous technological development. Each can be shown to be an improvement over its predecessor in accomplishing the end-in-view—tilling the soil. Each represents progress in this sense: it accomplishes the end-in-view better. This series of ends-in-view fits into the continuous life process in the same manner. This kind of change is an evolutionary development. To the institutionalist this evolutionary development is progress, and that is all that progress means. There are no Ultimate Ends or Absolutes involved in the process.

This whole way of viewing progress is also related to the institutionalist's concept of human nature and of social organization, which also are Darwinian in nature. Classicism does not develop a concept of evolutionary progress because of the concepts of human nature and social organization upon which the classical theory rests. Price is studied as a manifestation of human actions. These actions are part of a discrete series which are always directed toward re-establishment of a disturbed static equilibrium. Progress, being the accumulation of money funds, fits into the general Newtonian frame of reference in which traditional theory is couched. Accumulation represents a quantitative increase but no evolutionary change. It calls merely for shifts in a mechanically established equilibrium. The institutionalist does have a concept of evolutionary progress because his attention centers on that aspect of culture which is subject to evolutionary development—technology. That is why institutionalism is Darwinian.

VI

SUMMARY AND CONCLUSION

The discussion has now reached a point where some final comparisons and conclusions may be drawn. As the reader may recall, the aim of the inquiry has been to exhibit the difference between classical and institutionalist economic theory with regard to change. It has been contended that of the many differences which have been claimed to exist between these two types of economic theory, their difference with regard to change seems to be the outstanding one. In fact it is contended that the difference between the concepts of change of the two schools goes a long way toward explaining other differences.

Classicism developed in the eighteenth-century climate of opinion which was completely dominated by the work of Sir Isaac Newton at the beginning of that century. Newton sought and outlined an explanation of the movements of the stellar universe in mechanical terms. His laws of gravitation and mechanics provided an explanation of repetitive mechanical motion. The so-called natural laws by which the physical universe was governed were tools for analyzing a repetitive mechanical motion.

But Newtonianism spread and influenced all thought in the eighteenth century, including that of moral philosophy from which political economy split off. The moral philosophers sought those natural laws that governed the social universe. Such natural laws of social organization were conceived to be similar in their effect to Newton's laws of mechanics and gravitation. Thus the concept of mechanical and repetitive motion, peculiar to the Newtonian system, was drafted by the social philosophers to explain social phenomena. In fact the borrowing was so complete that early economists such as Adam Smith used Newtonian metaphors in explaining price changes. Prices were said to "gravitate" about the normal or "natural" price.

So great was the effect of this way of thinking that it influenced the totality of economic thought not only of the early formulators but of the present ones as well. This influence has been exhibited in the concepts of human nature, social organization, and progress. But more can be said than this. All of these concepts are interrelated, and together demonstrate the influence of Newtonian change in the over-all thought of the classical economist.

Fundamental to the whole classical pattern of conception of change is the concept of human nature. The Newtonian character of classical thought largely finds expression in the concept of a hedonistic human nature. By virtue of the assumptions of hedonism, classical economic theory was able to conceive change as being of a mechanical and repetitive nature. So conceived, all action is stimulated by an imbalance of pleasure and pain, and all action is aimed at a re-establishment of a lost equilibrium. Economic life itself is conceived as a discontinuous series of actions always aimed at achieving a state of balance or equilibrium. On the individual level of generalization, economic science is the study of individual satiation. Analogies using Robinson Crusoe and other hyper-imaginary, solitary, and primitive men are nothing but the study of how these individuals undertake action in order to reach a state of balance through achieving satiation. This whole way of viewing human activity is Newtonian, for it seeks to demonstrate the mechanical and repetitive nature of human gyrations. No cumulative change takes place in human activity—only a loss of satiation and a movement back toward satiation.

But this is by no means all there is to the matter, for this concept of human nature is directly related to the classical concept of social organization. To the classicist, society is the aggregate of all of the social molecules of the three major types: landlord, capitalist, and laborer. Through the mechanics of the price system their individual hedonistic actions become meshed into an economic system. But this price system has all the characteristics of Newtonian mechanics. Change takes place in the quantities of prices, but not in the system itself. Economic dynamics consists of the study of foreign elements, such as population growth and invention, as the influence of these foreign elements is registered in quantitative price movements. But always behind these price movements are the hedonistically directed movements of the economic molecules, landlord, laborer, and capitalist. In other words, prices register the quantitative changes in the sensations of these molecules. It is because of a change in the intensity of sensation of the conglomerate mass of economic molecules that changes in prices are brought about. Likewise, a re-establishment of equilibrium is accomplished by the fact that while one type of molecule, say labor, is repelled by a particular price change, another type, say capital, is attracted by the same price change. In brief, the price system as a social organization merely registers these changes in the total economic structure.

But these changes in price are subject to a repetitive and mechanical change. They do not bring about a change in the substance of the economy. Every change away from a presupposed norm (equilibrium) is immediately counteracted by an opposing force, so that the economic molecules are directed back toward the equilibrium (best) arrangement of things. The compelling force always at work is self-interest. The classical concept of normal price or natural price around which market or real price gravitates is a wholly Newtonian concept. Economic society, being the price system, is subject to this type of Newtonian change and motion.

Likewise the classical concept of business cycles is only an application of this same concept of Newtonian change to the price system as a whole. The very idea that the price level is subject to repetitive and periodic fluctuations that can be measured with a high degree of mathematical nicety is Newtonian in origin, whether the seekers of the "true" business cycle are aware of the fact or not. In this view of things, society is a permanent structure composed of landlord, capitalist, and laborer, and economic change is nothing more than movements away from and back to equilibrium—which is nothing but a balance of sensations of pleasure and pain to the nth degree of nicety.

From this conception of permanent social organization the classical theory of progress follows. This theory of progress in no way damages the classicist's earlier formulations, despite occasional allusions to technological advance or progress. Since specific technological advances are subsumed under the head of "Disturbing Elements," it follows by a quick transposition of terms that general technological advancement becomes identical with pecuniary enhancement. In other words, progress is an enlargement of money funds. The assumption that with progress a larger quantity of pleasant sensation is realized, although not explicit in classical theory, is certainly implicit. In this fashion progress is tied to the hedonistic conception of human nature.

The institutionalist conception of change is Darwinian. This follows from the frame of reference of institutionalist theory. As was indicated in each of the three previous chapters, the institutionalist deals with economic phenomena as cultural phenomena. But culture is subject to a process of cumulative growth. Like that of the classicist, the institutionalist concept of human behavior is basic to his concept of economic change. As was shown in Chapter III, the institutionalist conceives the human agent as active—as doing something. Action is not predicated upon sensations; action takes place first and sensations are incidental to actions. But this conception of human nature is also related to the concept of culture. What kind of activity takes place? It is culturally conditioned activity.

This activity taking place within a cultural milieu reveals two distinct, but not unrelated, aspects. Some activity is of the nature of institutional behavior; that is, it is shaped by custom and habit enforced by the authority of myth and legend. This type of activity is subject to only gradual erosion. But all human activity is not of this nature. Continuity and cumulative development are apparent in human behavior. This second aspect of human behavior is instrumental or technological in nature. Action in this area is subject to a matter-of-fact evaluation in which only demonstrable fact is relevant. But because of this evaluative process, this activity is subject to cumulative development. It is this aspect of human activity that is registered in cultural growth.

To the institutionalist the development of technology is synonymous with progress. Progress is the continuity of technological development. That is what it means. Any other meaning, such as progress toward some transcendental end, is defined by institutional authority, whether religious, metaphysical, or cultural, and is therefore subject to discount on the ground of cultural relativism.

In brief, the reason institutionalism differs so radically from classicism with regard to change, and thus in total outlook, is because institutionalism is built on the concept, culture. This is evident in its conception of human nature, in its conception of social organization, and in its conception of progress. All are discussed as aspects of culture. It is culture that has a dynamic as well as a static element. The dynamic element of culture is what is subject to evolutionary development. This evolutionary development of culture is economic progress. Thus change, and not statics, is the very center of institutional theory.

Nowhere is the effect of the difference between the two schools clearer than in their concepts of the role of the market. To the classicist the market or price phenomenon is a reflection of human nature, for the market in equilibrium is nothing but that hedonistic balance toward which all human activity is directed. Human desires and wants become translated into price valuations in the market and thus become objectified. Through the market mechanism, human desires are equated, balanced, and matched off against one another. The psychological balance, so important to classical theory, is achieved through the gyrations of the market. The market is a precise regulator of resource allocation that allocates in such fashion that resources are channeled into types of production that assure a maximization of want satisfaction. Raw materials are so channeled into production that the resultant product is in quantity and quality precisely what the totality of consumers desire. The end product is equated with a maximization of want satisfaction which is assumed to be equivalent to the "good society." Thus, in classical theory, there is a meliorative trend to price movements in the market which works toward this preconceived good end—maximization of utility.

The institutionalist does not look upon the market as the handiwork of a hedonistic human nature. A money economy is a cultural phenomenon that may have its antecedents in tribal gift giving or the giving of sacrifices to a deity who is expected to reciprocate by spectacular fêtes of mastery over the elements. Whatever its origin and evolution, certainly the market system is not a reflection of human nature. Rather, what is commonly called human nature is a product partially of the market system. Individuals born and culturally conditioned in a money economy develop pecuniary habits of thought. They learn to view things economic in pecuniary terms. Undoubtedly, to the institutionalist, the market is significant in the economic development of western society, but since it is not a product of a hedonistic human nature, it does not have the same significance for the institutionalist that it has for the classicist.

To the institutionalist, as was earlier contended, progress is the product of technological advance. Western society has two outstanding features, technological advance and business. The market, or the business aspect of that culture, can at best permit this technological progress and at its worst may inhibit it. In other words, the market may deter the achievement of maximum human welfare. This is diametrically opposed to the position of the classicist. Nowhere is this position more clearly stated by an institutionalist than by Veblen in his *Theory of Business Enterprise.*

These differences between the two schools are a product of the same evolutionary development upon which the institutionalist places so much stress. The concept of change itself has been subject to cumulative development as man's tools of analysis have improved. Social Newtonianism certainly represented a progressive development over the conception of change being under divine control. Social Darwinism, as manifested in the concept of cumulative cultural growth, is an improvement on social Newtonianism. This change in the concept of change itself is likewise continuous, as is all technological development, for each development was dependent upon all that had gone before. In this sense institutionalism is a later development of economic theory, and in this sense it represents progress.

BIBLIOGRAPHY

Ayres, C. E., *The Divine Right of Capital,* Boston, Houghton Mifflin, 1946.

———, *The Problem of Economic Order,* New York, Farrar and Rinehart, 1938.

———, *Science the False Messiah,* Indianapolis, Bobbs-Merrill, 1927.

———, *The Theory of Economic Progress,* Chapel Hill, University of North Carolina Press, 1944.

———, "Fifty Years' Development in Ideas of Human Nature and Motivation," *American Economic Review,* XXVI, No. 1, Supplement.

———, "The Co-ordinates of Institutionalism," *American Economic Review,* XLI, No. 2, Supplement.

Baykov, Alexander, *The Development of the Soviet Economic System,* Cambridge, Harvard University Press, 1947.

Beard, Charles A. and Mary R., *The Rise of American Civilization,* Vol. 2, New York, Macmillan, 1930.

Becker, Carl, *The Heavenly City of the Eighteenth Century Philosophers,* New Haven, Yale University Press, 1932.

Berle, A. A. and Means, Gardiner C., *The Modern Corporation and Private Property,* New York, Macmillan, 1947.

Böhm-Bawerk, Eugen von, *Karl Marx and the Close of His System,* New York, Augustus Kelley, 1949.

———, *The Positive Theory of Capital,* New York, G. E. Stechert and Co., no date.

Boulding, Kenneth E., *Economic Analysis,* New York, Harper, 1948.

Bowman, Mary Jean and Bach, George Leland, *Economic Analysis and Public Policy,* New York, Prentice-Hall, 1949.

Brown, J. F., *Psychology and the Social Order,* New York, McGraw-Hill, 1936.

Bryson, Gladys, *Man and Society; The Scottish Inquiry of the Eighteenth Century,* Princeton, Princeton University Press, 1945.

Bury, J. B., *The Idea of Progress,* London, Macmillan, 1928.

Childe, V. Gordon, *What Happened in History,* New York, Penguin Books, 1946.

Clark, John Maurice, "Round Table Conference on Institutional Economics," *American Economic Review,* XXII, No. 1, Supplement.

Clark, J. B., *The Distribution of Wealth,* New York, Macmillan, 1902.

———, *Essentials of Economic Theory,* New York, Macmillan, 1915.

Commons, John R., *Institutional Economics,* New York, Macmillan, 1934.

———, *The Economics of Collective Action,* New York, Macmillan, 1951.

Cooley, C. H., *Human Nature and the Social Order,* New York, Charles Scribner's Sons, 1902.

Copeland, Morris A., "Economic Theory and the Natural Science Point of View," *American Economic Review,* XXI, No. 7.

———, "Institutional Economics and Model Analysis," *American Economic Review,* XLI, No. 2, Supplement.

Daugert, S. M., *The Philosophy of Thorstein Veblen,* New York, Columbia University Press, 1950.

Dewey, John, *Human Nature and Conduct,* New York, Modern Library, 1930.

———, *Reconstruction in Philosophy,* Boston, Beacon Press, 1948.

———, "The Theory of Valuation," contributed to the *International Encyclopedia of Unified Science,* and published as separate pamphlet, Chicago, University of Chicago Press, 1939.

Dillard, Dudley, *The Economics of John Maynard Keynes,* New York, Prentice-Hall, 1948.

Dixon, R. A., *Economic Institutions and Cultural Change,* New York, McGraw-Hill, 1941.

Dixon, R. A. and Eberhart, E. Kingman, *Economics and Cultural Change,* New York, McGraw-Hill, 1938.

Dixon, Roland B., *The Building of Culture,* New York, Charles Scribner's Sons, 1928.

Dorfman, Joseph, *Thorstein Veblen and His America,* New York, Viking, 1940.

Ely, R. T., "Round Table Conference on Institutional Economics," *American Economic Review,* XXII, No. 1, Supplement.

Ferguson, John M., *Landmarks of Economic Thought,* New York, Longmans, Green, 1938.

Gambs, John, *Beyond Supply and Demand,* New York, Columbia University Press, 1946.

Gruchy, Allan G., *Modern Economic Thought; The American Contribution,* New York, Prentice-Hall, 1947.

Halévy, Élie, *The Growth of Philosophic Radicalism,* London, Faber and Faber, 1949.

Hamilton, Walton, *Price and Price Policies,* New York, McGraw-Hill, 1938.

———, "Institution," *Encyclopedia of the Social Sciences,* New York, Macmillan, 1932.

———, "Organization, Economic," *Encyclopedia of the Social Sciences.*

———, "The Development of Hoxie's Economics," *Journal of Political Economy,* XXIV, No. 9.

———, "The Institutional Approach to Economic Theory," *American Economic Review,* IX, March, 1919.

Haney, Lewis H., *History of Economic Thought,* New York, Macmillan, 1936.

Hart, A. G., *Money, Debt, and Economic Activity,* New York, Prentice-Hall, 1948.

Hicks, J. R., *Value and Capital,* Oxford, Oxford University Press, 1946.

Hofstadter, Richard, *Social Darwinism in American Thought 1860-1915,* Philadelphia, University of Pennsylvania Press, 1944.

Hollander, Jacob H., "The Development of Ricardo's Theory of Value," *Quarterly Journal of Economics,* August, 1904.

Homan, Paul T., "An Appraisal of Institutional Economics," *American Economic Review,* XXII, No. 1.

Hoxie, R. F., *Trade Unionism in the United States,* New York, D. Appleton, 1917.

James, William, *Psychology,* Cleveland, World Publishing Co., 1948.

Jevons, W. S., *The Theory of Political Economy,* London, Macmillan, 1888.

Kallen, Horace M., "Behaviorism," *Encyclopedia of the Social Sciences.*

Keynes, J. M., *The General Theory of Employment, Interest and Money,* London, Macmillan, 1938.

Kierstead, B. S., *The Theory of Economic Change,* Toronto, Macmillan, 1948.

Laski, Harold J., *The Rise of European Liberalism,* London, George Allen and Unwin, 1947.

Malinowski, Bronislaw, *Magic, Science and Religion,* Glencoe, Ill., Free Press, 1948.

Malthus, T. R., *Parallel Chapters from the First and Second Editions of an Essay on the Principle of Population,* New York, Macmillan, 1914.

———, *Principles of Political Economy,* Boston, Wells and Lilly, 1821.

Marshall, Alfred, *Principles of Economics,* London, Macmillan, 1930.

Mill, John Stuart, *Principles of Political Economy,* London, Longmans, Green, 1909, Ashley ed.

Mitchell, Wesley, *The Backward Art of Spending Money,* New York, McGraw-Hill, 1937.

———, *Lecture Notes on Types of Economic Theory,* New York, Kelley, 1949.

Mumford, Lewis, *Technics and Civilization,* New York, Harcourt Brace, 1934.

Parker, Carleton H., *The Casual Laborer and Other Essays,* New York, Harcourt, Brace and Co., 1920.

Pigou, A. C., *The Economics of Welfare,* London, Macmillan, 1924.

Randall, John H. Jr., *The Making of the Modern Mind,* Boston, Houghton Mifflin, 1926.

Ricardo, David, *The Principles of Political Economy and Taxation,* London, J. M. Dent and Sons, 1937.

Robbins, Lionel, *The Nature and Significance of Economic Science,* London, Macmillan, 1935.

Roll, Eric, *A History of Economic Thought,* New York, Prentice-Hall, 1946.

Samuelson, Paul A., *Economics,* New York, McGraw-Hill, 1948.

Say, Jean-Baptiste, *A Treatise on Political Economy,* Philadelphia, J. B. Lippincott, 1863.

Schumpeter, Joseph A., *Capitalism, Socialism and Democracy,* New York, Harper, 1947..

Smith, Adam, *An Inquiry into the Nature and Causes of the Wealth of Nations,* New York, Modern Library, 1937.

Stark, Werner, *The Ideal Foundations of Economic Thought,* New York, Oxford University Press, 1944.

Sweezy, Paul M., "Keynes, the Economist (3)," reprinted in *The New Economics,* ed. by Seymour Harris, New York, A. Knopf, 1948.

Taylor, Horace and Barger, Harold, *The Modern Economy in Operation,* New York, Harcourt Brace, 1949.

Tarshis, Lorie, *The Elements of Economics,* New York, Houghton Mifflin, 1947.

Toynbee, Arnold, *Lectures on the Industrial Revolution of the Eighteenth Century in England,* London, Longmans, Green, 1908.

Veblen, Thorstein, *Absentee Ownership and Business Enterprise in Recent Times,* New York, Viking, 1945.

———, *The Engineers and the Price System,* New York, Viking, 1947.

———, *Imperial Germany and the Industrial Revolution,* New York, Viking, 1946.

———, *The Instinct of Workmanship,* New York, B. W. Huebsch, 1922.

———, *The Nature of Peace and the Terms of Its Perpetuation,* New York, Viking, 1945.

———, *The Place of Science in Modern Civilization and Other Essays,* New York, Viking, 1942.

———, *The Theory of Business Enterprise,* New York, Charles Scribner's Sons, 1935.

———, *The Theory of the Leisure Class,* New York, Modern Library, 1934.

Waddington, C. H., *The Scientific Attitude,* Great Britain, Penguin Books, 1948.

Warden, Carl J., *The Emergence of Human Culture,* New York, Macmillan, 1936.

Weber, Max, *The Theory of Social and Economic Organization,* New York, Oxford University Press, 1947.

White, Leslie, *The Science of Culture,* New York, Farrar Straus, 1949.

White, Morton G., *American Social Thought,* New York, Viking, 1949.

Wilson, Thomas, *Modern Capitalism and Economic Progress,* London, Macmillan, 1950.

Wissler, Clark, *Man and Culture,* New York, Thomas Y. Crowell, 1923.

Woodworth, Robert S., *Psychology,* New York, Holt, 1934.

Wooton, Barbara, *Testament for Social Science,* New York, Norton, 1950.